Principles of Leadership

"Too many leaders plan for success and loaf to failure."

– Dr. Jack Hyles

Principles of Leadership

by
Dr. Jack Hyles

September 25, 1926–February 6, 2001

Pastor, First Baptist Church
Hammond, Indiana
1959–2001

Chancellor, Hyles-Anderson College
1972–2001

Superintendent, Hammond Baptist Schools
1970–2001

Superintendent, City Baptist Schools
1978–2001

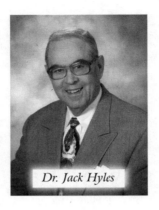

Dr. Jack Hyles

Copyright 2003
HYLES PUBLICATIONS
Hammond, Indiana

ISBN # 0-9709488-9-1

1st Printing–February 2003

Scriptures taken from the King James Bible.

CREDITS:
Layout: Linda Stubblefield
Proofreading: Elaine Colsten, Martha Gilbert,
and Julie Richter
Cover Design: BerylMartin

To order additional books by Dr. Jack Hyles,
contact:
HYLES PUBLICATIONS
523 Sibley Street
Hammond, Indiana 46320

Website: www.hylespublications.com
E-mail: info@hylespublications.com

About
Dr. Jack Hyles

JACK HYLES BEGAN preaching at the age of 19 and has pastored for over half a century. At the time of his death, First Baptist Church had a membership of over 100,000 with a high year of 20,000 conversions and 10,000 baptisms. For many years the church has been acclaimed to have the "World's Largest Sunday School." During Dr. Hyles' ministry the First Baptist Church's property value increased to over $70,000,000.

In an average week, Dr. Hyles counseled over 150 church members, managed two Christian elementary schools, one Christian junior high school, two Christians high schools, and the largest fundamental Baptist Bible college in America along with his regular pastoral duties and sermon preparation.

Dr. Hyles left his mark on Christianity, and his legacy remains through the books he has written, through the sermons he has preached, and through the lives he has changed. He is the author of 49 books and pamphlets, exceeding over 10 million copies in sales. He preached over 60,000 sermons; many of his sermons are available on tape.

Dr. Hyles' experience covers numerous evangelistic campaigns, Bible Conferences, etc. He preached in virtually every state of the Union and in many foreign countries.

Principles of Leadership

The annual Pastors' School, started by Dr. Hyles, attracts thousands of preachers from every state and many foreign countries.

Lest anyone should be confused with all that Dr. Hyles accomplished, he did so by spending more than 20 hours a week in prayer and the study of God's Word. He was a firm believer in the surrendered Christian life and the necessity of the Holy Spirit to accomplish much good for God.

A Note from Hyles Publications

IN AN ATTEMPT to continue the ministry of our beloved former pastor and leader, Dr. Jack Hyles, we are in the process of assembling materials taught by Brother Hyles from a multitude of sources. No, Brother Hyles did not leave behind dusty manuscripts waiting to be discovered in desk drawers and closets. However, he did leave behind a wealth of materials from his taped sermons available since 1970. He left behind videos of his weekly Saturday night classes where for many years he taught as many as 800 preacher boys. He left behind classic chapel messages he preached at Hyles-Anderson College. He also left behind series of lessons from his Wednesday evening studies. Of course, he left many messages around the nation at churches where he spent a great part of his life ministering to others.

We, at Hyles Publications, gleaned leadership helps for this book from several of these sources. Even so, as we began work on this book of leadership principles, we soon realized we had not even begun to touch the surface of all that Brother Hyles taught on just that one subject.

Because Brother Hyles is no longer available to read the

Principles of Leadership

manuscripts we are compiling, only a minimum amount of editing is being done. Most of the editing is for clarity, continuity, and to delete some of the repetition in taped messages that was a classic trait of Brother Hyles.

Much of what Brother Hyles left behind in taped form can only be shared with others by means of the printed page. With that thought in mind, please have mercy on us as we work to continue the ministry of Brother Hyles.

Contents

	Foreword 11	
1.	Leading Yourself 13	
2.	Principles of Leadership 23	
3.	The Priorities of Leadership 31	
4.	Principles of Mental Discipline 45	
5.	The Principle of Quietness 49	
6.	The Principle of Waiting 59	
7.	How to Treat Your People 67	
8.	Principles for Building Successful Relationships 73	
9.	The Importance of Counseling 81	
10.	Preparation for Counseling 83	
11.	Choosing Advice to Give 95	
12.	Basic Principles of Counseling 101	
13.	Kinds of Counseling 105	
14.	Principles for Public Speaking 115	
	Conclusion 137	

"It's not how high you can jump;
it is how near you are to the same height
all the time."

– Dr. Jack Hyles

Foreword

MANY SELF-HELP books are available on the market that will list principles and the needs of leadership. Seldom will a book address the real aspects and qualities of leadership. The secular business world has defined leadership in a way that allows them to promote success in business and corporate profits. The entertainment industry has marketed leadership in such a way as to allow Hollywood the greatest potential of notoriety and self-exaltation. The reality of leadership for the child of God must be defined by the Saviour in His earthly walk while leading great multitudes.

One of the most recognizable evidences of leadership of any fashion is answered by the question, "Is there a following?" If no one is following, it isn't difficult to see that the leader is not leading anyone. *"And Jesus went about all the cities and villages, teaching in their synagogues, and preaching the gospel of the kingdom, and healing every sickness and every disease among the people. But when he saw the multitudes, he was moved with compassion on them, because they fainted, and were scattered abroad, as sheep having no shepherd."* (Matthew 9:35, 36) These verses give us one of many accounts proving Jesus had a following; Jesus was a leader.

A leader would rather do the work than get the title. Accomplishment is always better than title or position. I once called the name of one of the most famous churches in America, a church with history and tradition. I asked who

Principles of Leadership

could tell me the name of the person who pastored the church. Less than ten percent of the crowd knew his name. I then called the name of a relatively new work that had experienced phenomenal growth. I asked who could tell me the name of the pastor. All of the people present knew the name. This example is to illustrate that it is far better to do the work than to get the position. One man had done a great work and was well-known. The other man had accepted the pastorate of a church with a great tradition and history; and consequently, he held a great position but was not so well-known. Real leaders are not desirous of position or fame. They are desirous of an opportunity to do something for God and for others.

I have often defined leadership as being one who collects ideas from followers, compiles them, and sends each follower a copy. To that end, this book on principles of leadership has been compiled.

Chapter One

Leading Yourself

"HE THAT IS *slow to anger is better than the mighty; and he that ruleth his spirit than he that taketh a city."* (Proverbs 16:32) This verse does not say that the person does not get angry. A person cannot be slow to anger unless he has anger. An individual cannot come back from where he has not been. No one can be slow to anger unless he is on the way to becoming angry. What God is saying in this verse is to be able to be angry. That is what it also means in Ephesians 4:26a where the Bible says, *"Be ye angry, and sin not...."*

There are times when a person should get angry. The person should make sure that he decides when those times will be and when his will, not circumstances, tells him to get angry. A leader does not react to anger; he acts with anger. Anger should never be a reaction; it should always be an action. In other words, anger is a decision made by the one who possesses the will to be angry.

America is destitute for men. I hesitate to write this, but I am never so aware of just how destitute America is for men as I am around election time. It is amazing how difficult it is to find a **man** running for office. Males can be found who are running for office, but it is hard to find a real man running for office. In the same way, many of America's pulpits are destitute for real men. Leadership on the part of men is almost extinct. Truthfully, the average man is led by his wife, and it's not because she is a bossy, dictatorial Jezebel.

[13]

Principles of Leadership

Rather, it is because she is married to a wimp. After all, someone has to take care of the checkbook, and if he doesn't, she has to! Someone has to take care of seeing that the family doesn't go bankrupt, and if he doesn't, she has to! Frankly, I would rather that young ladies stay single the rest of their lives than to marry a man she will have to claim as a deduction for the IRS.

When I was a young man, strong leaders were almost commonplace. We looked up to men like General Douglas MacArthur, General Charles de Gaulle of France, and Winston Churchill of England. Franklin Delano Roosevelt, who was liberal, was still considered a strong leader. Even the Hitlers and Mussolinis, though they were wicked men, were strong leaders.

In my search for true leadership, I come to an old warrior whose hair is like the snow on the mountain peak; his shoulders are drooped; his brow is furrowed; his hands are palsied; and his voice is shaky. I say, "Sir, you are not long for this world. You have been a leader now for many, many years. May I ask you a question? What was your greatest accomplishment while you were in leadership? Was it when you killed a bear or slew a lion with your bare hands? Was it when you took the five stones and a slingshot and felled the mighty Goliath? Was it when you ruled a nation in power? Was it when you conquered the enemies' cities? Was it the leading of a nation through two rebellions or insurrections? What, dear aged one, was your outstanding achievement in leadership?"

The old warrior strokes his grizzled beard, thinks a while, and he finally speaks, "None of these. My great time of leadership was not in killing the bear or the lion or even Goliath. It was not in leading a nation through two revolutions and two insurrections, or leading a great nation from the throne of Israel in Jerusalem. The time that I led the

Leading Yourself

best was at the door of a cave. My enemy, Saul, was sleeping at the door of the cave. At the time, I was running for my life because he was trying to kill me. There he was—the man who had hurled javelins at me and vowed that he would kill me. As I pulled my sword, I was encouraged to pierce his breast. I merely cut off a little bit of the hem of his garment and let him live.

"I also did a great job of leading when my son, Absalom, led a rebellion against my forces, and I had to flee from Jerusalem. A man who was a member of the house of Saul named Shimei began to curse at me. He threw stones and cursed not only me, but my servants. My servant, Abishai, begged me to allow him to kill Shimei. I said, 'No, let him alone, and let him curse.'

"The third time that I showed myself as a great leader was during the rebellion itself. I could have led those loyal to me into battle. I could have fought against my son. I could have killed my son."

"May I ask you another question, sir? You said that these were your greatest times of leadership. Whom did you lead, King David?"

"I led myself."

When a person is able to lead himself, he is performing the greatest act of leadership known to mankind. If a person never learns how to lead himself, he will never be qualified to lead anyone else. Many a young man pictures himself leading a congregation or even a great congregation like First Baptist Church of Hammond, Indiana. Some picture themselves leading a college like Hyles-Anderson College, but they will never lead a church or college until they perform the greatest act of leadership known to man, and that is the act of leading themselves. Consider the leadership qualities of these recognized leaders:

- Saul could lead a nation, but he could not lead him-

Principles of Leadership

self, and the nation of Israel fell.
- Alexander the Great led a nation until he became a slave to alcohol; then he could not lead himself. In his slavery, he could no longer lead the nation of Greece.
- Solomon led an empire until he couldn't lead himself; when he couldn't lead himself, the empire crumbled.
- Samson could lead a nation until he could not lead himself. He could not lead himself in the lap of Delilah, and he lost his power to lead nations.
- Daniel never led a nation, but he led himself. Some men never lead an army, but they lead themselves.
- Joseph never led an empire; but when Potiphar's wife tried to seduce him, he led himself by fleeing temptation.

No man will ever amount to much as a leader of men until he leads himself. Why is leading yourself such an accomplishment?

1. Your follower does not want to be led. He wants to follow. Greater than Douglas MacArthur leading in the Far East, greater than Dwight Eisenhower or General George Patton leading troops in the European theatre, greater than General John Pershing leading the American Expeditionary Forces in World War I, greater than General Ulysses Grant leading the Union troops, or General Robert E. Lee leading the Confederate troops is that kind of leadership where someone looks in the mirror and says, "I'll lead **you.**" I promise you, when I look in the mirror to shave myself every morning, I see a man.

When Mrs. Hyles once spoke in Pastors' School, she gave the number of days that I slept in past 7:00 a.m. In 50 years, I can count on one hand the number of times that I slept in. I have gotten in at 3:00 a.m., but I did not sleep in. I have gotten in at 5:00 a.m. and did not sleep in.

Someone once said to me, "Dr. Hyles, I wish I had that

Leading Yourself

kind of energy." It is not *energy*. I have wanted to sleep in time and time and time again, but I decided years ago that I may not be able to lead multitudes, but there is at least one fellow who is going to follow me, and his name is **Jack Hyles**.

 2. **Your follower wants to lead.** Not only do you yourself not want to be led, but your follower wants to lead you. At one point in my life when I decided to lose weight, I lost 65 pounds; my follower and I have not gotten along since. Of course, in order to lose that 65 pounds, I had to decide when and what I would eat. On a day when I knew I wasn't supposed to eat, I happened to be on an airplane. The stewardess offered me three choices for lunch. After she kindly listed what was available, I declined the lunch; but "my follower" said, "We'll take one of each."

 I said, "Shut up, Hyles. You will be my follower; I will lead you. A few salivary glands are not going to run my life. I will lead you."

 When the stewardess brought the meal for the gentleman sitting beside me, "my follower" said, "Look at what your neighbor is eating." I felt like I watched every bite he took.

 When I finally got off the plane, "my follower" and I went to the room where I was staying. We stumbled over cartons of Reese's peanut butter cups, Nutrageous, Snickers, Butterfingers, Almond Joys, and potato chips, popcorn, and 22 other miscellaneous snacks. My follower said, "We are going to have a good time!"

 I said, "Shut up and hush!" "We" ate a box of raisins. I decided when I was going to eat—**not** my stomach nor my salivary glands. America is bereft of men who can lead themselves because they cannot lead their glands.

 3. **You do not want to lead your follower.** A leader leading himself is not what most leaders have in mind.

Principles of Leadership

Leaders have in mind leading a deacon board or a great congregation of people. That kind of leader will fall flat on his face until he learns to lead the person he shaves in the mirror every morning.

"Yes," David acknowledged, "I killed Goliath, but that wasn't as hard as restraining myself when I had the opportunity to get back at King Saul. I led a kingdom; I ruled from a throne, but my great leadership was when I did not retaliate against Shimei or my rebellious son."

The question comes, "Dr. Hyles, you lead the largest church in America. Is that your greatest leadership accomplishment?"

"No, sir. When I was a junior high lad, I was elected president of the 800 students of our class. As the president, I was commanded by the activities director and then the principal to lead the conga line and ballroom dance with the secretary of the class in the gymnasium at the Boude Storey Junior High School. I'll be honest with you; I wanted to do it, and myself' asked, 'What's wrong with that? It will last only five minutes.'

"I said, 'Self, you know what's wrong with that.'

"I looked in the faces of the activities director and the principal and said, 'Jesus would not have me to dance. I do not believe that it is right.' "

That was a harder victory and a greater leadership than leading the largest church in America. Until a leader can handle that kind of leadership, he will not lead people.

In my senior year, my best friend and his girlfriend double-dated with my date and me. They decided to go to a nightclub and a movie on a Sunday night. I called my date's mother and father to tell them I was no longer responsible for their daughter. I told them she was going to a movie, and that I was going to church. I did not allow the peer pressure or a pretty girl to lead me. I led myself.

Leading Yourself

When my Uncle Harvey offered me enough interest in his business to make $250,000 ($2.5 million today), he stipulated that I would have to attend Southwestern Seminary and earn a doctorate. Myself said, "What's wrong with that? You will still believe the Bible. Think of all the money you could send to missions or how many churches you could start in America."

I said to myself, "You can rationalize all you want to, but you know it's not right to sell your soul for a quarter-million dollars. Sit still, and I will decide what to do."

I led myself. I did not let money lead me. When I looked in the mirror each morning in those days, I saw a man. When I look in the mirror now, I still see a man.

My mother was on her deathbed, and I was flying to a meeting. I called Hyles-Anderson College from the airport and asked for the clinic. The head nurse of the clinic answered the phone and said, "Brother Hyles, if you want to see your mother alive, you need to come now."

I answered through tears, "I made her a promise last night that I wouldn't cancel a preaching engagement. Would you put the telephone close to Mother's ear?" (Every Monday before I left the airport, I called Mama. The last words I always said to her were, "I love you, Mama.") I screamed as loud as I could, hoping that she would hear me, "I love you, Mama! I love you, Mama!" As I hung up the phone, I thought, "I can't get on that airplane. I just can't do it," but I did. Mama reared a man.

When I went to Hammond, the city had just had a mayoral election, and the mayor was on the board of First Baptist Church. The richest men in town attended First Baptist Church. Those men wanted to buy me off. A **man** cannot be bought! A **man** cannot be bought by denominations. A **man** cannot be bought by popularity or fame or money. A **man** is not for sale! A **man** decides to perform the

[19]

Principles of Leadership

greatest act of leadership known to mankind, and that is the act of leading himself. Only then will he be qualified to lead someone else.

The world is waiting for the man who controls himself and leads himself, but no one will ever lead a great crowd until he first performs the greatest achievement known to mankind—and that greatest of achievements is to lead himself. A leader must lead the most rebellious person he knows—himself. He leads the one person who does not want to be led—himself. He leads the person who wants to lead—himself. He also leads the person who does not want to lead—himself.

When I came to First Baptist Church of Hammond in Indiana, I soon learned that my predecessor was as different from me as from daylight to dark. He preached in scissor-tailed coats and striped britches. I loosened my tie and let it rip! He was an American Baptist; I was an Independent Baptist. His crowd rebelled against me, and he himself came back to Hammond to help them organize another Baptist church when First Baptist went through the 1960 split. Through the battle, I never once led the people away from him. Real men do not build themselves on the shoulders of other people. The leader who makes another person six inches shorter will not grow one inch. Though at first my predecessor was my enemy, his dad stayed with First Baptist Church. Dad Miller was what I call a man.

When he was ill, I went to visit him. He asked, "Young man, do you know why I stayed with you?"

"Not exactly," I replied.

"I stuck with you because you ain't got no rope for a backbone," he declared.

How about you, leader? What kind of backbone do you have? While you have the time and the opportunity and before you think you are the second coming of Billy Sunday,

Leading Yourself

take hold of yourself and decide that you are going to lead the man you shave. In so doing, you will prepare those to follow you later.

To be a real man, one must obey himself. He must develop his will in order to make his body and his mind obey his will. The most rebellious person to me is me. The leader, therefore, must obey his will. He must say to his body in the morning, "Get up!" He must sometimes say to his body, "You cannot eat now." Other times he must say, "You cannot eat that kind of food." He certainly cannot rule others until he can rule himself. That is why the wise man said in Proverbs 16:32, *"He that is slow to anger is better than the mighty; and he that ruleth his spirit than he that taketh a city."* Be a man!

"God will not do what we can do,
but He will do what we cannot
after we have done what we can do."

– Dr. Jack Hyles

Chapter Two

Principles of Leadership

JESUS SHOWED HOW He led; yet, He did so without trying to be a leader. Jesus did not tell the multitudes to follow Him; the people did so of their own volition. People followed Jesus because He taught, preached, and healed. They followed Him because they had witnessed the miracles He had performed. People follow a person because of the qualities they see in that person. For example, the disciples were convinced that Christ knew how to get ahold of God. They wanted to have or to learn what Jesus possessed in terms of prayer. *"And it came to pass, that, as he was praying in a certain place, when he ceased, one of his disciples said unto him, Lord, teach us to pray, as John also taught his disciples."* (Luke 11:1)

The key to being a leader is not in trying to learn how to lead, but in being what Jesus was. A leader needs to be many different things for many different people in many different circumstances.

1. **Leaders do not lead; they are followed.** *"Then saith he [Jesus] to the man, Stretch forth thine hand. And he stretched it forth: and it was restored whole, like as the other. Then the Pharisees went out, and held a council against him, how they might destroy him. But when Jesus knew it, he withdrew himself from thence: and great multitudes followed him, and he healed them all."* (Matthew 12:13-15) People follow someone who can lead them to where they want to go.

Principles of Leadership

A good example of that philosophy is illustrated by Pastors' School. Followers need a leader; but it is not the leader they will receive. Followers receive the influence of the leader.

In the Bible, the follower is always commanded first as to how he is to behave toward the leader. God always demands that the follower first be what he is supposed to be. God tells the employee to submit first. God tells the wife to submit to the husband first. Then, God commands and instructs the leader how to behave toward the follower.

When a follower finds a leader who tries to give him what he needs, that follower will be very careful to let his leader know how much he needs him. Followers should also be very careful to receive and respond to what the leaders believe they need.

2. Some leaders want people to follow them so that they can do great works. This kind of leadership is not real leadership. Too many preachers compare themselves to those who pastor great churches and wrongly assume that if they pastored the same number of people, they too could have great works. What that kind of leader needs to understand is that if he would himself perform great works, he would have the great numbers.

What made Lee Roberson a great leader was the fact that he built a great ministry, and as a result, people wanted to know how to do what he had done.

3. The leader who builds his ministry will build his people. "Use your work to build your people, not your people to build your work" is the philosophy by which I have lived.

Often, when I am preaching in another pulpit, I look out into the audience and spot a man who looks like he may work as a mechanic. I begin to think of the sacrifice he went through to come hear me preach. I think of the fact that he

Principles of Leadership

probably got up early that morning and went to work in a garage. After work, he rushed home just in time to clean up a little and get to church in time for the service. He probably did not even have time to sit down and have a good dinner before he came. Suddenly, I find myself in a loving mood, and I want to do my best to be a blessing to that man, as well as to the other people who came to hear me preach.

A leader must make certain that his followers do not determine his mood; rather, his mood should be determined by what his followers need. This characteristic is what makes a leader a leader. That thought leads me to say that the determining factor of my emotions is the needs of others. Too often a leader becomes angry because he is frustrated or aggravated, rather than because those who follow him need him to be angry. This type of leadership is selfishness; moody people are those who have no control of their emotions. As a result, those kinds of leaders are not able to be what their followers need them to be. The person who determines the mood is the leader.

Rather than allowing my emotions to control me and cause my people to suffer, I control my emotions with my will for the sake of what my people need me to be. I decide when I will be happy, angry, or unhappy. If I allow my emotions to be controlled by outside sources, I am not a leader. I am a follower because others can control my moods. Let me explain. People often tell me that my preaching during the summer months is the best preaching I do. I do not know whether or not that statement is true, but I do know that the summer months are the most difficult months a pastor faces because so many people are away. This fact is especially true at First Baptist Church of Hammond because many of the Hyles-Anderson College students are gone during the summer months. What do I do? I work even harder

Principles of Leadership

to be inspired during those months when the crowds are not overflowing the auditorium. I do not allow the circumstances to control my mood. Too many preachers allow their audience to determine their mood, rather than their being in the mood they need to be in for the sake of their people.

In the same respect, many preachers allow the crowds, during the holiday season to determine their moods. Because many church members visit family during the holidays, the leader rebukes those who are in church because the crowd is down. Tragically enough, they are scolding the very ones who are there rather than the ones who are not! That kind of behavior on the part of leadership not good. A leader must control his moods.

I have studied myself carefully so that I know what causes my moods to change. For instance, I know what causes me to be discouraged. Because I know what causes discouragement, I guard myself from anything that may discourage me. The reason that I guard myself is because I have great crowds of people who need me. They do not need a discouraged me; they need an encouraged me. They do not need a depressed me; they need me to be upbeat. I, therefore, try to prevent any kind of stimulus coming into my heart or mind that would even remotely bring discouragement. I refuse to associate myself with that which brings discouragement; I feed myself only that which encourages me.

Leaders are often guilty of saying, "That makes me mad!" Nothing is supposed to provoke anyone to anger, least of all a leader. A leader gets angry only when he has decided to get angry. I refuse to allow any person or situation to determine my emotional state. I refuse to allow outside circumstances to make me unable to give people what they need from me. I am responsible to help others, so I cannot allow others to control my spirit. That responsibility leads me to my next point.

Principles of Leadership

4. A leader cannot serve God without serving people. If a leader lives to serve, his conscience will be directed to do what he does for others rather than for himself. When a leader is good to others, he is being good to Jesus. That attitude will make a leader conscience-oriented toward doing what Jesus would do rather than what he wants. Most people who have what I call "broken" consciences will make their choices based on what they selfishly want.

If a leader wants to have a strong conscience, he will get busy living for others. Serving God is not what a leader does **not** do; rather, it is what the leader does do. The reason a leader preaches against sin and stops wrongdoing is to strengthen himself to serve God by serving others. A leader's conscience will be healthier as he begins to live his life totally consumed by the needs of others. I am trying to be what my people need me to be. I then pass on to my people that which has influenced me. As their leader, that is all I can do. I am to be to my people what they need me to be; consequently, I take what I have seen and heard, and I pass it on to my people.

For that reason alone, a leader must be careful what he chooses to read. A leader will become what he reads, but that is not all. The people he leads will become what a leader reads. When I read what I ought to read, I do it for the sake of my people, not for my sake.

A leader must be careful in choosing the people with whom he associates. When I choose the people with whom I fellowship, it is for the sake of those who follow me. I must not be careless about it because my choice will influence the people I love and want to influence properly. If I am what my people need, and if I have nothing of myself, I must collect it from those with whom I fellowship. I must be careful that they pour into me the right ingredients so I will be the right conduit through which flows good and right, instead of bad and wrong. If a leader chooses to associate with the wrong crowd, that association not only influences the leader, it will also influence the people whom he leads. When someone influences a leader in a negative way, he will in turn, influence his followers wrongly. If a leader is to give the people who follow him what they need, he must receive what he needs. A leader must be careful what he hears. I need to be careful that what I hear will help me, so that it will then help others.

Therefore, if the people who follow me become what they need to become, I must be careful of the influences on my life. I am preparing myself to be with the people to whom I minister. If I am going to be to my people what they need, I must be sure that I am influenced in the direction they need to be influenced. I am not doing this for my own sake, but for theirs. For a leader to be all that he can be is selfishness. For a leader to be all that he can be because it will influence others is unselfishness. Most adults have people who follow them. Children will largely become what their leaders influence them to be, and that will be determined by what their leaders are influenced to be. If a leader is going to influence others properly, then he must govern the influences in his life. A leader must be careful what he reads, what he hears, and with whom he associates.

5. **A leader cannot serve his people without persevering.** In my office, I have posted the words, "Never despair; but if you do, work on in despair." When I hurt and despair, I must continue to work on. When I fret and despair, I must keep going. When I doubt, I must continue to work on and keep going.

Great leaders persevered when others quit. The only difference between Dr. Lee Roberson and a thousand other preachers is that when he despaired, he stayed and faced the same problem that caused others to leave. Those who persevere and endure are called leaders. The leader hurts like the follower, but he does not quit like the follower.

Let Your Principles Decide!

The making of a decision is only half as important as the process it took to make the decision. Throughout my life, I based my personal decisions on five main principles:
- I will not allow anyone to meddle with my preaching.
- I will not make money an issue in my ministry.
- I will be a friend to my friends.
- I will base every decision on right and wrong and not on its outcome.
- I will be loyal to principles and not to institutions.

Likewise, I urge every leader to formulate lasting principles by which to live.

"What you are is more important than what you can do."

– Dr. Jack Hyles

Chapter Three

The Priorities of Leadership

Acts 1:1 says, *"The former treatise have I made, O Theophilus, of all that Jesus began both to do and teach."* Jesus did what He did in the power of the Holy Spirit. Luke 3:16 and other passages tell us that Jesus was filled with the Holy Spirit, and those verses confirm what He did in the power of the Holy Spirit. Just as Jesus began to do His work in the power of the Holy Spirit, His people are to continue that work also in the power of the Holy Spirit.

John 14:12 states, *"Verily, verily, I say unto you, He that believeth on me, the works that I do shall he do also; and greater works than these shall he do; because I go unto my Father."* This verse is saying that what Jesus started, He will finish.

John 20:21 says, *"...as my Father hath sent me, even so send I you."* This verse means that God sent Jesus Who started the work, and now He sends us, and we are supposed to finish His work. The same meaning can be applied to I John 4:17, *"...as he is, so are we in this world."* Jesus started, and we are supposed to continue His work.

Allow me to take some principles from the life of Jesus as a leader and show how we are supposed to apply them to our lives and to our own places of leadership. I call these the priorities of leadership.

I guess that if anything in our generation is lacking it is

Principles of Leadership

real leadership. Somehow too many think that because they have a title, they have a right to "run the show." Too many want authority without knowing how to handle that authority. Let me illustrate an example of real leadership.

A pastor, in one of the most difficult areas of America to build a church, picked me up at the airport for a meeting. He always met me with fine questions and subjects to discuss. It took me off guard when he asked, "Dr. Hyles, the first thing that I'd like to ask you is what do you think is most important about leadership?" When I didn't have a ready answer, he said, "Think about it a few minutes and give me what you think is most important about leadership." He kept me talking, and after I listed five areas, he said to me. "You should teach that at Pastors' School. In fact, you should teach that to your church people."

I said, "I believe I've mentioned most of these things."

He said, "Do you mind if I teach these things to my people?"

I said, "Not at all." After I got to my room, I made these notes. I had just ad-libbed and had spoken extemporaneously while riding in the car.

In my words, the most unlikely people are leaders. One day in a Bible class at East Texas Baptist College, I picked up a little paper called the *Sword of the Lord*. I began to read sermons by a man named John R. Rice, whom I had never seen. I had a mental picture of what I believed he must look like—6'4", 240 pounds, a giant of a man. By the way he wrote in the *Sword of the Lord*, I thought he must be the meanest man in the world. I thought he must eat nails for breakfast and little children for supper. Still, I literally fell in love with the man because he was against everything. Before I ever met him, he became one of my heroes.

One day I was at a pastors' meeting in Dallas, Texas, on a Monday morning, and someone sitting beside me said,

THE PRIORITIES OF LEADERSHIP

"Do you know who is here?"

When I said, "No," he said, "Dr. John R. Rice is here." I began to look for a man who rose above the crowd like a King Saul or a Goliath. After all, that was how I thought Dr. Rice would look as a leader. I couldn't find him. I only saw one unassuming potbellied fellow standing in the corner whom I didn't know, and I did wonder who he was.

Finally the moderator stood and said, "Gentlemen, we have Dr. John R. Rice as our guest today. Let's bow our heads for prayer."

I bowed my head, closed my eyes, and waited for that booming voice I had imagined. He began speaking like he was at a funeral, saying, "O God, O God, come in power."

The voice was coming from the direction of the strange-looking fellow I had wondered about earlier. I opened my eyes, looked over to where I thought he was, and he was the man praying! Dr. Rice just did not look like what I thought he would.

I was asked, by someone who was taking a poll for the secular press, to list the five greatest men of this generation and the last one, and they stipulated, "We want greatness, not necessarily religious. We want the names of men who are of great stature or statesmen."

I listed John Rice; Bob Jones, Sr.; Winston Churchill; Douglas MacArthur; and J. Edgar Hoover. I had no problem putting John R. Rice on the same par as these men. I honestly believe with all my heart that John R. Rice could have been President of the United States. In fact, I do not know of a single man in our generation who is a preacher who could have been President of the United States except for John R. Rice. I never knew a man who knew about as many things as John R. Rice. He possessed the most brilliant mind I ever knew in my lifetime.

Years ago, I heard about a giant for God named Lester

Principles of Leadership

Roloff. When I met him, I found a little, old, bald-headed boll weevil! I will never forget the time he took off his coat to talk about health food. As he said, "Look at me tonight," he held his arms up like a fighter! I don't think I ever knew a man who could cause men to follow him like Lester Roloff did. I have discovered that the normal traits often associated with leadership are not usually representative of true leadership.

1. **Copyable.** A leader is someone who is followed, and in order to be followed, that person has to be followable or copyable. Jesus was copyable. Jesus chose 12 apostles, and these men spent three to three and a half years with Him. They watched Him do His work. When He went to Heaven, He told them to do what they had seen Him do. They continued doing His work; that is being copyable.

Sad to say, some great preachers in this nation have not had a great influence on this nation because they have not been copyable. For instance, there is only one R. G. Lee. When R. G. Lee died, R. G. Lee died. When I die, there will probably be hundreds of little Jack Hyles all over this country. I will never forget the day I asked R. G. Lee to write the introduction to my book, *The Hyles Church Manual*. He agreed, but he wanted to read it first. When Dr. Lee gave me back that manuscript and his introduction, he cried nearly uncontrollably. I asked him why he was crying, and he said, "Because I wish I could have read this book 35 years ago. If I had read this book then, I would have baptized 3,000 people instead of 300 people a year."

One day I commented to Dr. Bob Jones, Sr., "Aren't we glad there's a John Rice?"

He answered, "Aren't we glad there's just one? It would be terrible to have two John Rices going all over this country telling people what is wrong with them. One *Sword of the Lord* is wonderful; two would be terrible!"

The Priorities of Leadership

If you are going to be a successful leader, someone has to follow you. They have to walk where you walk, which means that you have to be copyable. I have often said that a leader should be a stencil who runs off copies of himself.

If you visited First Baptist Church of Hammond on a day when I was not behind the pulpit and Brother Colsten was conducting the service, you would know what I was like because of the way the service was operated. In the same way, you can walk into Hyles-Anderson College, and though I do not have an office on site and only speak there once a week and occasionally for another purpose, you would know what kind of man I am by attending chapel. One of the reasons why it is easy to copy me is that simplicity is easier to copy than profundity. Be copyable.

I'm always impressed when a son wants to be what his father is. I'm always impressed when the daughter of a preacher's wife wants to be a preacher's wife. I'm always impressed when a carpenter's son wants to be a carpenter or when a plumber's son wants to be a plumber. I'm always impressed when followship wants to copy leadership.

2. Transparent. A transparent leader is a readable leader. Let me illustrate. Dr. Bob Jones, Sr. said that people would oftentimes ask him, "Have you ever thought about divorcing your wife?"

He said, "I never have; I never have. I've thought about choking her to death a few times, but not divorcing her." I believe his answer showed the transparency of Dr. Bob Jones, Sr.!

I was in Indianapolis for a meeting with Dr. John Rice. When I arrived, Dr. Rice was already in the restaurant. I walked in at 5 o'clock in the evening, and Dr. Rice was eating scrambled eggs, so I ordered the same thing. He was just sitting across the table from me not saying very much. I knew he was thinking because Dr. Rice always tapped his

Principles of Leadership

fingernails when he was thinking.

"Dr. Rice," I asked, "what are you thinking about?"

He commented, "Aren't women funny?"

"Dr. Rice," I asked, "did you and Mrs. Rice have a little tiff today?"

He said, "No, a big one."

I liked his answer because it was a sign of greatness—not the fact that he had a tiff with his wife, but the fact that he admitted to having a disagreement.

I will never forget the first time I saw Lester Roloff doing his radio broadcast. He had invited me to come and preach for him in Corpus Christi. I walked in and said to the receptionist, "I'm here to see Brother Roloff."

She said, "He's broadcasting." Of course, broadcasting tends to be very, very formal. He was live on the air when he noticed me waiting, and he hollered, "Come on in!" I walked in to the broadcast booth, and he wasn't wearing shoes or socks. In fact, he had just taken a nap and was still wearing his pajamas. That's the first time I ever saw Lester Roloff broadcasting!

I believe there's something transparent about a leader, and leadership lets others see through the windows.

3. Mystique. By the word *mystique*, I mean that there should be a little something mysterious in a leader. A child should never be able to totally figure out his dad. When Sarah called Abraham, "Lord," I don't think he was wearing his shorts, barefoot, eating popcorn, and watching the football game on Saturday afternoon.

I preached to the Hyles-Anderson College preacher boys, "Let your people know you have feet of clay, but never show them your feet." People should know that a pastor is human, but that pastor should not display his humanity. Of course, a pastor has weaknesses; but he cannot display those weaknesses.

The Priorities of Leadership

How then can a leader have both transparency and mystique? A leader can have both transparency and mystique because a leader is always learning. If people want to explore their leader, he must always be exploring. A leader can be transparent and teach people everything he knows, but the next time they see him he should know something else. A leader has to constantly be exploring, learning, and thinking. I heard someone make the statement, "I wish I knew what he knows." When I heard the statement, I didn't care for the statement, and I still don't care for it. Rather, I prefer hearing, "I wish I could find out how he finds out. If I could find out how he finds out, I'll find out what he knows."

The leader must always be learning. True leadership does not say or reveal everything he knows on any given subject because someone might ask him a question when he finishes. Leadership has to always be reading. Leadership has to always be exploring. Because of that necessity, leadership cannot spend an excessive amount of time with followship.

I travel often on the same plane with athletic teams. I have noticed that the best coaches do not sit with their players on the airplane. Once I traveled with the Chicago Bulls when Dick Motta was the team coach. I noticed that the players sat together; Coach Motta sat alone. Occasionally, Coach Motta would go to where the players were and chat with them, but he always went back to his seat.

I believe the main reason for young people getting divorces is that the mystique has been lost. The couple has nothing left to study. They have no more challenges and no more to explore. A real leader can never be totally explored because he is always exploring. If a person happens to learn all his leader knows today, the person won't know all that his leader knows tomorrow. That follower will want to come back and see what his leader has learned. This means that a leader has to spend a lot of time alone. Why? Because he is gathering and exploring, learning new things, reading new things, thinking new things. This is one reason why I refuse to read books for personal pleasure; I read to learn what I feel will help me help my people.

Every once in a while I hear a comment like, "I wish I had a lot of original ideas like he does." That person doesn't have a lot of original ideas; he spends a lot of time thinking. Those same ideas are available to anyone, and anyone could have them if he would think. A leader must meditate a lot, read a lot, study a lot, and be alone a lot. And to possess this trait of mystique, a leader must often be alone with God.

I never heard Lester Roloff speak but what I felt like he had been with God since I had last seen him. Mystique cannot be created. A person creates mystique by having explored something since he was last explored; therefore, to have mystique a person must spend some time alone and a lot of time alone with God. The leader has to be alone while others play. The leader must be alone with God while others are with each other. Only then can he possess that wonderful trait of leaders called mystique.

4. Servitude. Somehow some preachers have gotten the idea that their people are supposed to serve them. No! Leadership is made for service. Jesus said that the servant is greatest of all. He said that Jesus came to minister to people, not to have people minister to him. *"For even the Son of man came not to be ministered unto, but to minister, and to give his life a ransom for many."* (Mark 10:45) The liberals have stolen the word servant and use it too often, but the truth is, a leader is supposed to be a servant. I, Jack Hyles, am supposed to serve my people.

The Priorities of Leadership

I study so I can serve my people. I prepare my sermons and Bible studies so I can serve my people. When I counsel, I am serving my people. I want to be a servant to my people.

Personally, I think the idea of preachers being served by their people evolved from the country days when the preacher was poor, the churches were small, and the depression was upon America. Most of the preachers did not get paid monetarily, or they were paid very little. Rather, the church people brought vegetables, milk, buttermilk, butter, eggs, and meat; they spoiled him with foods. Let's transfer that philosophy to today. If some pastors don't receive a new car on their anniversary, they get upset.

I am not here for my church people to spoil me; I am here to spoil my people. My job as a pastor is to serve my people. Every pastor's job is to serve his people. Leadership is not commanding; leadership is service. Quite frankly, what I hate the most about leadership is that I do not like to be a boss. If I ever had to say anything cross to my staff, I returned to my office and wept a while. I want to give everyone what he wants.

The greatest danger of leadership is when people love a person and grant that person authority. If he doesn't watch out, he can abuse that power. If a leader isn't careful, he will get to thinking that he is the final authority on every area. If individuals will obey their leader all of the time and follow him all of the time, he can become a little pope.

At this writing, for 40 years now, I have been counseling with people and pastoring churches. I have seen the percentages of how different actions and different decisions turn out. All I give when I counsel is the best percentage. If I have watched people come to a crossroads in life, and the people who go one way turn out better 80% of the time, and those who choose the other way turn out better 20% of

Principles of Leadership

the time, I advise the person with whom I am counseling to take the 80% way. Certainly, I am not God. It does mean that a person would be very, very wise to listen to someone who has experience and has watched people go both ways. That is the reason why I never ask the person with whom I am counseling to always do what I say. Instead, I ask the person with whom I am counseling to give me veto power. Even if I know there is a bridge out one way because I have seen some choose that way, I will still not tell a person what to do. I simply say that I would like to veto that choice. I never tell a man where to go or whom he should marry, I just ask to have veto power.

I believe every young person should give his pastor and his parents (if they are spiritual parents and care about him), veto power about major decisions like choosing a marital partner. I personally do not believe an individual should marry someone if I know a reason why he should not.

You say, "Who do you think you are, God?"

No, I think that for 40 years I have been watching young people make certain decisions, and I believe in percentages. I can tell another what the percentage is if he chooses to go a certain way. All I want with my people is the power of influence. Any time people give a person power, it can be easy for that leader to usurp that power and authority and abuse it. That is why in leadership the leader should be a servant.

5. Identification. Identification means that the leader must relate to the follower, and the follower must identify to the leader. An individual once said, "Brother Hyles, do you know what you do to me?"

I answered, "What?"

He said, "First you make me want to do it. Second, you make me feel like I can do it."

I loved his statements! "You make me want to do it, and

The Priorities of Leadership

you make me feel like I can do it, too." Followers must be able to relate to leaders.

Please don't misunderstand this next illustration. I'm going to word this where it may seem a little suggestive, but it wasn't.

A church lady said, "Brother Hyles, you've been my pastor now for a long time. Could I shake your hand?"

As I said, "You surely can," I took her hand and shook it.

While shaking her hand, she said, "That's the first time I ever shook your hand." She went on to say, "This is the first time I've ever talked to you other than to say 'hello' or 'good morning', but I feel like I've known you all my life. We have built fires in wood stoves together. We have gotten stuck in the snow together. We have lost our hair together. We have brushed our teeth together. So many of the little homespun illustrations that you've used are exactly where I've been. Preacher, I know you real well."

That is called transparency. A leader and his followers learn to identify, and the more things that they can do together the better they know each other, and the more things they can do in their minds. The distance is not very great between the leader and the follower. Yes, the leader and the follower have to stay just a bit apart so they can keep learning, but not so far apart that they cannot identify with each other.

One of the most important statements I ever made from the First Baptist Church of Hammond pulpit was, "I must walk with man to find his problems, and I must walk with God to find their solutions."

People come by my office and ask, "Brother Hyles, would you give me advice on such and such…?" and tell me the situation. Very often, I ask the person, "What do you think?"

Many times the person will say what I think, and I won't have to tell that person what to do.

I say, "That's tremendous. I would do the same thing myself." Because of waiting on the person to think through his situation, I haven't had to exercise any power or authority over him.

True Leadership

Years ago, Dr. Bob Jones, Sr., one of the five greatest men of this generation, came to our house. He walked into the living room at 1540 Hilltop in Garland, Texas, on a Sunday afternoon. A little three-year-old girl named Becky, with hair as gold as a gold piece, toddled over to him and looked up at him. Dr. Bob Jones, Sr., said, "Hello there. What is your name?"

She said, "Becky."

He asked, "How old are you?"

She said, "That many," and held up three fingers.

He said, "Oh, you're so pretty."

A little while later he asked, "Do you like candy?"

She said, "Yes, sir."

He reached into his pocket and pulled out a little package of assorted Life Savers® and gave them to Becky. Three-year-old Becky reached into her breast, took out her heart, and gave it to Dr. Bob Jones, Sr. From that moment on, he was her favorite preacher. (I was a little jealous.) When we would have Dr. Rice to our house, Becky would say, "I like Dr. Rice, but I would rather have Dr. Bob Jones, Sr." She loved Dr. Bob dearly. When Becky gave him her heart, she never forgot it. She never forgot that package of Life Savers®.

Ten years passed. Dr. Bob never came to our house

THE PRIORITIES OF LEADERSHIP

again, and he never saw Becky again. In the meantime, we moved to Hammond. I was invited to Bob Jones University to preach for several days. While I was there, Dr. Bob came to the President's Place in the dining hall. By that time, he was senile, and he was living alone in his little apartment on the Bob Jones campus. He had lost his memory; I had heard him use the same illustration nine times in the same sermon. Dr. Bob came up to me and said, "Dr. Hyles, I didn't get to hear you in chapel today; but I heard you on the radio, and I felt like hitting the mourner's bench."

So I said, "Well, why didn't you, Dr. Bob?"

He grinned. Then asked, "How's Becky?" I was shocked because he had not seen that girl in ten years. In fact, he had only seen her one time when she was three years old. Though he had lost his memory, he remembered Becky! "How's Becky?" he asked again.

"Dr. Bob," I asked, "do you remember Becky?"

He said, "Well, of course, I remember Becky with her golden hair."

"Dr. Bob, how could you...?"

"How could I forget her?"

I said, "Dr. Bob, you are still her favorite preacher."

Tears streaked down his battle-scarred cheeks. His voice quivered as he said, "I am?"

When I said, "You're still her favorite preacher, always have been," he could hardly speak.

The following Saturday morning at breakfast time, the doorbell rang at the Hyles' house. I went to the door, and the postman had a package. He said, "I have a package for Becky Jan Hyles." (I had mentioned to Dr. Bob that she'd be 13 on Saturday. He said, "I can't believe she'll be 13.")

I said, "Becky, it's a package for you."

Becky ran to the door, grabbed the package, opened it, ran back into the kitchen, and yelled, "Daddy! Daddy!

Principles of Leadership

Guess what? It's from Dr. Bob Jones, Sr."

What was it? A carton of assorted flavor Life Savers®. He never forgot; he never forgot Becky.

I'm not sure that when you describe the greatness of his leadership, but I believe that instance may have been one of the best illustrations of true leadership. Ralph Waldo Emerson penned such appropriate words when he wrote,

> *So nigh is grandeur to our dust,*
> *So near is God to man,*
> *When Duty whispers low, Thou must,*
> *The youth replies, I can.*

Being a great leader is a great responsibility. If you have a little child who calls you Mommy or Daddy and has to obey you, you have a tremendous responsibility. Study and study and study and while you are studying, give consideration to five words: copyable, transparent, mystique, servitude, and identification.

Chapter Four

Principles of Mental Discipline

DOLPH SCHAYES, THE basketball player, always looked at a picture of a man who was to guard him and built up a mental image of his opponent in order to prepare himself for the game. Dolph saw his opponent as that which was keeping him from becoming a success. That kind of mental discipline made Dolph Schayes the leading scorer in the NBA.

All kinds of outside stimulus cause all kinds of changes in a person's mind. Especially is this fact true in the ministry; however, a pastor cannot allow himself to change from one mood to another. A leader must be predictable. Many people change preachers like they change barbers. A pastor is allowed only one bad mistake—such as botching a wedding or a funeral. A pastor is allowed little variation. Quite frankly, a pastor is seemingly always on trial. Mental discipline is very necessary.

1. A leader must be an atmosphere setter. Most preachers "ride" the atmosphere rather than creating it. To create the right kind of atmosphere, a leader will analyze his good days and recreate them. In the same respect, he will analyze his bad days and do all in his power not to recreate them. Too many leaders allow their days to be days of chance, with no thought of calculation. A wise leader will

Principles of Leadership

figure out the ingredients for success and failure and apply them to his ministry.

2. A leader must know how and what stimulates him. He cannot fake joy, compassion, or sorrow. He must know and choose what makes him joyous or compassionate or sad. A leader cannot turn on the tears, but he can turn on what turns on the tears.

A leader must know what makes him happy, what makes him sad, what makes him thankful, and what makes him worshipful. Former Indiana University coach, Bobby Knight, and former Chicago Bears coach, Mike Ditka, were known as hotheads; however, they were not the hotheads people believed them to be. Rather, they were calculating men who effectively used their show of temper. Bobby Knight planned on intimidating the officials during the course of a game.

3. A leader must find what acts as a stimulus for him. A leader should know what people stimulate his thinking. In the same way, he should know what thoughts to think. I choose my thoughts according to what kind of mood I want to be in. I don't let thoughts capture me; I capture them.

4. The leader must choose his tasks. He will decide what he is going to do. Rather than allowing his emotions to control him and cause his people to suffer, he controls his emotions with his will for the sake of what the people need him to be.

5. The leader must decide what mood the task requires. The determining factor of a leader's emotions is the need of others. Too often a leader gets angry because he is frustrated or aggravated, rather than because those who follow him need him to be angry. This kind of leadership is selfishness. Leaders who are up and down or moody are those who have no control of their emotions. Those kinds

Principles of Mental Discipline

of leaders are not able to be what their followers need them to be.

6. **The leader needs to choose the proper stimulus to bring the proper mood.** Just as a cook has a cupboard full of ingredients with which to cook, a leader should have a cupboard full of ingredients to put him in the appropriate mood for whatever the situation warrants.

7. **The leader will give himself to that proper stimulus.** He will allow that stimulus to dictate to him. Instead of saying, "Isn't it good to be a Christian?" he will say, "It surely is good to be a Christian!"

8. **The leader will know how to set aside the proper stimulus.** Do not always use the stimulus. Use it when the crowd needs the stimulus, not in small groups or with friends. Be yourself.

For a leader to be predictable, he must learn to have mental discipline. The leader who possesses mental discipline will be able to meet the needs of his people.

"You can destroy your chance
to do the talking you are supposed to do
by doing the talking
you are not supposed to do."

– Dr. Jack Hyles

CHAPTER FIVE

The Principle of Quietness

MY DEFINITION OF a principle is something that normally works. If 90 percent of the people get the same results from a certain course of action, then I feel like a leader is wise to give this advice. Relying on principles will save a leader more heartache than anything in the world. Isaiah 30:15 says, *"...in quietness and in confidence shall be your strength...."* The leader has to observe a principle of quietness—there is a time to be quiet. These times of quietness prepare the leader to meet the needs of his people. In the same respect, no one in a congregation can understand his leader's problem; therefore, the leader must go to God.

Times to Be Quiet:

1. When a leader wants pity, he should be quiet. Fifty percent of the people who come for counsel want pity, not counsel. Most of the people who make an appointment with a leader come to see the leader for help, not to help the leader. A leader will not lead for long if he seeks pity or sympathy—publicly or privately. No one can fully understand another's problem.

A leader forfeits his right to help others when he shares

Principles of Leadership

his problems with his people. When a leader shares his problems with people, he is bypassing the One Who truly understands. The truth is that leader is implying that God alone is not sufficient to meet his personal needs.

Most of the Hyles-Anderson College graduates who make serious mistakes make them in this area of facing problems. A leader should not burden his church members, nor should he burden his wife with the problems. I maintain that if a leader has to be boosted up, he has no right to be in the pulpit. The leader must learn the truth of the song, "Take your burden to the Lord and Leave It There."

The person who seeks pity seldom receives what he desires because so many others are also seeking pity. Instead, that person must hang onto God. After all, the person with a burden can ask any number of people to pray for him, but he still must carry his burden. A person will come closer to receiving sympathy by keeping silent. The leader must take care of his people's burdens and carry his own.

2. When a leader disagrees with another, he should be quiet. Most disharmony would disappear if people were quiet when they disagreed. An opinion doesn't always have to be given.

3. When a leader feels he needs to search out facts about an accusation against him, he should be quiet. The leader automatically lives in a glass house. The average leader wants to disprove false accusations, but God did not call a leader to refute false accusations. The leader's job is to help others. Strength always helps weakness.

When a leader faces criticism, he should direct the conversation away from the criticism. A leader cannot afford to talk about his problems. Oftentimes when a fellow preacher calls me with a problem and leaves his number, I can hardly ever get through to him. Most of the time, he is on the phone talking to anyone who will listen to his problem.

[50]

The Principle of Quietness

If a leader lives under the clouds, he will not be able to lift his people above the clouds. I cannot help you if I am burdened down with me. Neither can I lead my church if I know what everyone has to say about a certain incident. In these areas, I need to be quiet.

4. **When a leader's advice is not sought, he should be quiet.** I have lived by the motto, "I do not want to display my advice; I want to use my advice."

5. **When a leader knows the conversation will hurt him, he should be quiet.** No one wants to be hurt. Likewise, a leader should never place himself in a position to be hurt. He cannot help others when he is hurt, wounded, and bleeding. This is one good reason not to hang around with negative people. A leader must keep his mind positive.

6. **When a leader knows he can hurt someone, he should be quiet.** I have lost all confidence in some people, but I have determined they will never know it. What good would it do an individual for me to say, "I have no confidence in you"? Why should I add to a person's hurt? It takes more manhood to restrain yourself than to exert power. If a leader would ever get a hold of that truth, he would be quiet more.

7. **When a leader knows his advice will not be heeded, he should be quiet.** Troubles often start because a leader wanted to talk. Since it takes two to argue, common sense says that most arguments begin when one person will not be quiet. Unfortunately for those needing the help of a leader, "Unsought advice is seldom heeded," is too often true.

8. **When a leader does not want a situation to be known, he should be quiet.** I have learned that the sentence which contains the most wasted words in the English vocabulary is, "Don't tell anyone this...." I knew two moth-

ers who had preacher sons who had sinned and had to leave the ministry. One of the mothers told four ladies in a prayer group about her son's sin. The other lady told no one. Guess which son is back in the ministry? The son whose mother told no one is, of course, the son back in the ministry.

A leader should get to the point where he has talked to God so much about his burdens that he feels like he must have talked to everyone about them.

Situations to Avoid in Leadership

1. **Do not want to know who your enemies are.** The leader is the only person who can destroy himself. Others can only provoke him to self-destruction. Of what value can it be to know the names of people who disagree with those in leadership? The church people need the preacher more than the preacher needs the church.

Dr. John R. Rice taught me a valuable principle about enemies in the ministry. He said, "My opponent does not have to be my enemy." Through the years, I have had many opponents. I am glad to say that I am no one's enemy.

2. **Do not let the crowd go unfed because of one disgruntled person.** Do not continually glance toward the person you believe has something against you. Why not thank God for the 499 people who are for you rather than the one who seems to be against you?

3. **Do not be curious about what your enemies are doing or saying.** You would be surprised how small enemies look from 100 feet above them. I have learned that I can win more people than those can who become angry with me.

4. **Do not ever tell your side of the story.** First, your friends won't believe the accusations against you. Secondly,

The Principle of Quietness

your enemies will not believe your version. Thirdly, there is too much else to do for the cause of Christ than to spend your time defending your action. Lastly, you cannot combat venom with venom.

Enemies possess no logic; you will not change them by trying to use logic. An enemy's main problem is hatred. Do not give free publicity to those who are against you. Don't allow them to have a forum through you. You will also plant seeds of doubt when you defend yourself.

5. Do not talk when attacked. Generally, the guy who hits second gets penalized. You cannot win the fight when attacked; people are always for the underdog. As soon as I encounter a bad problem, I find someone else who needs my help. Soon I forget my own personal problem.

I live by the principle of giving everyone at least a ten percent leeway. Let me explain. If I hear that someone criticizes me, it does not cause me to lose my confidence in that person. Instead, I feel like maybe he had a moment of weakness.

6. Do not socialize on the spur of the moment; plan your socializing. I believe one of the most dangerous statements in the world is, "Why don't you come over tonight?"

The Pastor's Heart

One day the load was especially heavy, and the burdens were many. I had so many appointments that night, and to be quite frank, I rebelled a little bit at having to solve the problems of others when I had so many myself. After counseling with many people, it was about midnight. As I started to go home, I had the following thoughts. Please read the following poem very carefully.

Principles of Leadership

"I have a burden, Pastor, that
I'd like to lay on you."
I listened, tho he never knew
I had a burden too.

I took a tearful look toward mine;
Then his came into view.
'Twas plain to see my burden was
The larger of the two.

I saw his load alongside mine,
And, tho they both were real,
The yoke he bore was made of wood,
And mine was made of steel.

To him I said, "Come unto me;
I'll gladly carry thine":
Then whispered unto selfishness,
"But who will carry mine?"

I softly laid my burden down
To help him his to bear,
While knowing that my heavy load
I'm not allowed to share.

I'll help him with his burden, then
Regain mine after while,
When I will sigh and weep once more,
While now I force a smile.

I felt the CHAINS OF BONDAGE till
A CAPTIVE came to me.
He bade me help him break the bands,
And aid him to be free.

The Principle of Quietness

I saw the fetters binding him,
And felt a pity pain.
For his were made of little rope,
And mine of heavy chain.

I laid aside my heavy chains,
So he, my help, could borrow.
I'll help free him of bondage now,
And think of mine tomorrow.

A DOUBTER knocked at study door;
I had an urge to groan,
"Why bring your pebble doubt to me,
When mine is made of stone?"

I smiled at him and listened, while
Believing in my doubt.
I laid it down reluctantly,
And feigned about a happy shout.

I sat ALONE in darkened room,
And felt a shadow's knife.
Another came to share with me
Some darkness in his life.

As I compared my night with his,
His dark possessed a lack.
For his was just an evening shade,
While mine was midnight black.

I slowly laid my nighttime down,
To help him seek for light.
I'll tread my dimming path again,
When I have made his bright.

[55]

Principles of Leadership

A TROUBLED SOUL came to my door,
A problem to confide.
I had a problem, too, that day;
'Twas hard for me to hide.

My problem was a mountain steep,
And his was just a hill.
My problem was an ocean wide,
And his, a tiny rill.

Yet, 'tis my lot to fill his need,
And put mine on the shelf.
For I must lay my heartache down,
And hide it from myself.

He told me of a broken heart,
While mine was breaking too.
I told him of a mending God
Who maketh all things new.

He told me of his thirsty soul;
I gave him living water.
He said he was a broken vase;
I told him of the Potter.

Another came when I was SICK
To say he had the flu.
His fever was a hundred-one,
And mine a hundred-two.

Another came when I was FAINT,
To say that he was weak.
Another came when I was DUMB,
To say he could not speak.

The Principle of Quietness

Another WEEPING SEEKER came,
For me, his tears to dry.
I went alone and wiped my eyes,
Then told him not to cry.

Another came when I was TIRED,
To say he needed rest.
I lifted him with my weary arms,
And tried to give him zest.

AND NOW, IT'S LATE, and all have gone,
Each one to his abode.
So I must find my problems, and
Regain my heavy load.

Where is the burden I had borne?
I had it while ago!
Where is the problem I must solve?
I left it here, I know!

Where is the darkness I once knew?
I now see only light.
The chains, the tears, the pains, the fears,
Are nowhere now in sight!

I cannot find my broken heart!
Where is my fevered brow?
I have a song! the tears are gone!
I cannot find them now!

My sickness, now, hath turned to health!
And trust replaceth fright!
Assurance covers all my doubts;
My darkness now is light!

Principles of Leadership

I heard a voice from Heaven say
"My child, 'tis always true:
When you take care of others' needs,
I will take care of you."

Read this poem over and over again. Never let what people say determine what you, the leader, says. Always plan what you say.

Chapter Six

The Principle of Waiting

No matter who you are, others who are under your authority are being influenced by that which you decide to do. Your choices are not going to determine just your future, but also the future of all of those over whom you have influence. A leader is responsible for what happens to his followers. Every evil that falls upon them will be a part of the results of those choices. If the leader does well, his people will be blessed; if the leader does evil, his people will suffer. Therefore, I follow the principle of waiting in decision making. A good motto for the ministry is act swiftly, but do not decide swiftly. The leader needs to take his time in deciding what to do, then take swift action. The following are times to wait:

1. **The leader should wait before performing marital counseling.** The chances are that most people asking for marital counseling will soon be reconciled. Most wounds heal themselves. In the days prior to having the powerful antibiotics of today, a person who was sick had to "pass the crisis." Some people rush to the doctor too quickly; a resistance to the antibiotic is built up in the body.

That principle has caused me to wait 48 hours in all but the most extreme cases. Two-thirds of the couples who request appointments for marital counseling do not come.

Principles of Leadership

2. The leader should wait concerning the hiring of employees. Many of the church splits in America are caused by employees. I have waited up to three years before hiring staff members. I recommend always waiting at least three months before making a decision to hire an individual.

An employer who hires quickly will eventually hurt himself and his people. I suspect that hiring too quickly is the biggest mistake that pastors make.

3. The leader should wait before firing someone. If the leader hires right, he will never have to worry about firing someone. Firing is caused by improper hiring. I have not fired anyone in 41 years. If I hired the wrong person, I share in the crime. Firing someone deeply affects many people, including the wife and the children, all of whom will be uprooted. I believe that firing carelessly is wrong and immoral. It is wrong for innocent people to suffer because the leader hired the wrong person.

I have found that when a staff member leaves, other church members will follow him or leave the church. I have also learned that some employees are worth their salaries, even though they may do little or nothing, because of the tithes of their followers.

4. The leader should wait before spending money or making a purchase. A leader should always get three bids before purchasing any large item for the ministry.

5. The leader should wait before disciplining a person. I call immediate punishment "mob lynching." Having to administer punishment is often the fault of the leader. Many followers would not be guilty of infractions if the rules and penalties were carefully explained. When such is not the case, the leader has also erred and has become a party to the crime.

The leader should never punish when angry. The leader should first cool off. This cooling-off period should not be

The Principle of Waiting

used as a way of evading or avoiding punishment. It should be used as a time when the leader can search his heart to be sure his motives for imposing the punishment are right and just.

Every child deserves the opportunity to explain why he did what he did, and then to be informed why he is being spanked, should that be the needed form of discipline. Nine times out of ten, if a child is spanked immediately, the person doing the spanking is angry.

Harsh words should be used only when the leader feels they are needed. Again, those words should not be spoken in anger. Though the leader may appear to be angry, his words should be used only when the leader deems it wise. Harsh words spoken in an outburst of anger or during a temper tantrum should never be a part of disciplining a person. Sharp words should only be used when both the words and the way in which they are spoken are purposely chosen for the good of the follower. *"He that is slow to anger is better than the mighty; and he that ruleth his spirit than he that taketh a city."* (Proverbs 16:32)

Punishment should never be vindictive. No person should be punished because he is offensive to the leader, because the leader has lost his patience, because he is not liked by the leader, or because the leader wants to get back at him. No punishment should ever be inflicted unless the main motive is corrective. *"...My son, despise not thou the chastening of the Lord, nor faint when thou art rebuked of him: For whom the Lord loveth he chasteneth, and scourgeth every son whom he receiveth."* (Hebrews 12:5, 6)

6. The leader should wait before accepting a resignation. Ask the person who wants to resign to wait and pray about his decision. I ask ladies who wish to resign to pray and wait one month. On the other hand, if it is a resignation that you want, take it immediately.

Principles of Leadership

7. **The leader should wait before tendering his resignation.** Unemployed preachers are not good employment prospects. God will lead you from where you are to some other place. Don't leave a place of service unless you have another place to go. Certainly, do not let a resignation be an option. I have found that most preachers resign when they are affected by discouragement. Discouraged people are those who have no control of their emotions. The discouraged person is not able to be to his followers what they need him to be.

8. **The leader should wait before mailing a letter of rebuttal.** Doing so will probably eliminate an exchange of words that need never have been shared! If the leader feels he must send a letter to someone, he should wait until he is sure there is absolutely no emotion involved. *"Be not hasty in thy spirit to be angry: for anger resteth in the bosom of fools."* (Ecclesiastes 7:9)

9. **The leader should wait before making a verbal rebuttal.** Don't be quick to express your opinion. Anger should not characterize a leader. A wise leader is not often angry. Anger is a tool to be used only when it is needed; therefore, it can only be used when planned. It is not good for a leader to be angry because it reveals the fact that his anger is not under the control of his will. I try not to use anger until I recognize the fact that it is totally necessary to use the tool of anger to accomplish a needed result. Let me explain.

A graduate of Hyles-Anderson College accepted a position as an assistant pastor at a church. Word came to me that the graduate was lazy. I met with him and tried to help him, but he showed no improvement. I decided to get angry. Though I did not "fly off the handle," I needed to employ the tool of anger to scare him and correct him. I made another appointment to meet with that graduate, and I real-

THE PRINCIPLE OF WAITING

ly "chewed him out." Certainly I did not correct him to hurt him or to get it off my chest. I used my anger to help that young man. I am happy to say that he changed and eventually became a successful pastor. Why? Because I chose by my will the tool of anger to help that young man. I do not get angry at the drop of a hat, but I use the tool of anger only when I am sure that it is needed. Too many people become angry so much that the use of anger is no longer an effective tool.

10. The leader should wait before disagreeing with loved ones. For instance, a real leader allows his wife to have her own opinions and friends. Because women are made to follow, they do not depend on logic as does a man.

11. The leader should wait before borrowing or building. The wise leader will never build a building just because he wants a new building. He builds for the Sunday night crowd, not the Sunday morning crowd.

12. The leader should wait before making a decision. When a leader is being rushed to make a decision, it probably means it is the wrong decision.

13. The leader should wait before selecting lay workers for key positions. The wise leader will seek references on the people he is considering for those positions.

14. The leader should wait before expressing his opinion. I don't like to express my opinion unless it is needed for someone to be helped. If an opinion is asked during casual conversation, especially then should the leader wait to give his opinion. The wise leader never has a lot of unplanned fellowship time.

15. The leader should wait before starting a new ministry. I did not teach personal soul winning for the first three years I was at First Baptist Church of Hammond, Indiana. I was more concerned with getting the wrong people out of leadership roles in the church. For instance, I

[63]

Principles of Leadership

decided who should be teachers in Sunday school classrooms, and some people teaching were not qualified. The wise leader will wait to start a new ministry until the people are ready for it. Plant seeds first by mentioning ideas and things to think about from the pulpit. Wait for the people to come with the idea for a ministry you have wanted to begin. The man who learns to prepare his people is a leader. The leader should be sure that his decision has totally matured before he acts upon it. The wise leader will also wait until the right man is available to fill the position that will naturally be created.

  16. **The leader should wait before fighting, whether fighting back or starting a fight.** My motto has been, "No defense, no attack." There is a great danger in fighting a battle. A leader can become so enchanted with fighting that he spends his entire life chasing the enemy. He loses sight of his vision of helping his people.

  17. **The leader should wait before making any rash statements when members leave his church.** Be a gentleman when members leave your church so that the door will always be open when and if they decide to return. Too often the leader is afraid that if someone disagrees with him, that person who disagrees is an automatic enemy. The leader can avoid ever becoming offended by:
   (1) staying in the Word of God,
   (2) not seeing criticism as being personal attacks, and
   (3) not wanting things or position.

If the leader's critic is his inferior, the leader should make an allowance that the critic has not been privileged to know what he knows. The wise leader will never retaliate toward those who try to offend him, who are unkind to him, or who criticize him.

The Principle of Waiting

Act; Don't React!

If the following points were followed in fundamentalism, 95% of the problems would be solved. All leadership should be premeditated and planned.
- Do not spend casual time with people who entice you to react.
- Do not read items or listen to items that make you react in your mind. For instance, I do not listen to call-in talk shows.
- Be oblivious to what makes you react when you must be around the action.
- Plan your reactions before the battles. A planned reaction is an action.
- Decide what reaction you will display in any given situation. Know what you will do when a crying baby interrupts a service. Know exactly how you will handle any type of disturbance before the it occurs.

Real tears cannot be faked, but if a situation calls for tears, a leader knows what will bring the tears.
- Learn to whom you can trust your reaction. I spend time with people whom I feel will not provoke me to say something I should not say. Some people are masters at getting information. Confidentiality is a great part of the ministry. Certainly a leader will know some information that no one else can know. This knowledge not only pertains to facts and talents, but it also pertains to knowledge of people and circumstances which he cannot divulge to any other followers.
- Learn to whom you cannot trust your reaction. The leader must then preplan the conversation in such a way as to steer clear of negatives that may cause him to react. The wise leader controls the subject but not the conversation.
- Let it be known that you do not participate in criti-

cism. Thus, you have an insurance policy against reacting wrongly.
- Do not live in unplanned situations. Live by schedule; allow that schedule to be your boss.
- Do not look for reactions from others. In so doing, too often you become the reactor. Many marriages suffer because the husband's dependence upon his wife's reaction determines how he should react. Leaders must make certain that followers do not determine their mood; the mood of the leader is determined by what their followers need. This trait makes a leader a leader.

Great leaders determine their responses on the basis of need, not on the basis of response to another's provocation. A leader will not allow his emotions to control him and cause his people to suffer; a leader will control his own emotions with his will for the sake of what his people need him to be. Leadership is not strength used; leadership is strength restrained.

Chapter Seven

How to Treat Your People

THE WISE LEADER discerns the way in which each person wants and needs to be treated and treats them in that way. In other words, assess each person's "language of love" and speak to that person in that language. The leader will be a better leader if he knows the heartbeat of each of his followers.

There is something about the human race that makes them want to do kind things for people if they do not ask for kindnesses. If a person asks, generally that request is the last thing another one wants to fulfill. A leader should never allow himself to be tainted by this philosophy.

Every individual wants to be treated with dignity, professionalism, and lovingkindness. Every person enjoys receiving compliments and receiving expressions of appreciation—especially publicly. In addition to these, the wise leader will:

- Inquire of his members about their family.
- Seek advice from members in their area of expertise. Strength will listen to and consider the advice of others. One of my preacher boys once said, "I'm old enough now not to need counsel or advice. I don't need to ask Brother Hyles what he thinks anymore. It is time I became man enough to make my own decisions." I call this statement a

Principles of Leadership

statement of weakness, for weakness cannot stand up in the face of counsel. Weakness must avoid counsel. Strength can stand counsel and insists upon receiving counsel. This does not mean counsel will always be taken, but it does mean that counsel will always be considered.

- Allow your members to seek advice from you.
- Offer your members the opportunity to help you.
- Use notes and letters as a way of building his people.
- Make statements such as, "You're a great guy."
- Honor your members' requests to share their burdens, and then pray for them.
- Give verbal reminders of the security that you offer them.
- Remind your members that they are team players.
- Use humor to help your members feel loved.

Observations

1. Every person is an individual and should be treated as an individual.
2. Every person needs all of the aforementioned assurances, but every individual needs at least one of these assurances more than all of the others.
3. Do not withhold legitimate expressions of caring that people need and crave.
4. Know the personality weaknesses of your members and what provokes them; then avoid those areas. When you know what makes someone upset, it is silly not to avoid that issue—especially if that area is not sinful. Bathe your people with love and tenderness, but have the intestinal fortitude to stand—no matter who is at the opposite end of the gun barrel. In other words, don't avoid the areas of sin. The wise leader will confront the

HOW TO TREAT YOUR PEOPLE

areas that need to be confronted.

5. Know your personality weaknesses, and avoid situations that expose them. If you have a temper, learn to control it. As I have mentioned previously, leaders must control their moods. Also, you are better off not to try to control your faults; rather, work hard to avoid situations that expose those faults.

6. Do not confide in your members. You do not have to tell someone your problems!

7. Give public appreciation, but do private scolding. A real leader wouldn't hurt any of his followers for the world. This happens to be a general policy I have tried to follow for years.

8. Do not let negative people control conversations. Some very good people, who are not gossips or unspiritual people, are negative. A leader can become depressed by negative people. Their glass is always half empty, never half full.

9. Do not allow yourself to be drawn into private skirmishes. As I said in the previous chapter, be an actor, not a reactor. Along this same line, I never open mail on a Saturday night, in case a crank letter puts me in a bad mood.

10. Do not get into a fight or disagreement with a member. If the leader must fight, he should choose the circumstances and not be led or provoked.

11. Do not collaborate with any deacons before a deacons' meeting.

12. Do not invite your people into your life; let them peek into your life. Every great man whom I have ever known has been transparent. He tried to hide nothing.

13. Do not disagree publicly with what people say. In fact, do not tell the people that you disagree with them.

14. Do not start a sentence with a negative. Do

Principles of Leadership

not make statements like, "I disagree," or "I can't see that," or "We don't agree on that." Instead, say "What about this?" If a leader does not tell his followers first that he disagrees with them, he may have an opportunity to convince them later.

15. Do not penalize the critic.

16. Do not criticize the church people, especially not to your wife. Beverly Joyce Hyles has not heard me say one negative thing about anyone in all these years.

17. Do not have a best friend in the church. The leader cannot have an individual best friend. The leader and his wife cannot have a couple as best friends. One of the great secrets of discipline is a proper closeness between the leader and his followers. The wise pastor will have no problem with jealousy among his people or his staff members because he should have a unique relationship with every person in his church.

18. Let your people know that you have feet of clay, but do not take off your shoes.

19. Insulate yourself against negative thoughts. Don't let yourself know much about any negatives. If you don't fight back, you do not need to know the negatives.

20. Isolate yourself. If God called you to preach, He will take care of you. Leadership is loneliness.

21. Always remember that you are a servant; your people are not your servants. The leader seeks to fill every need that he sees. The wise leader sees every need as a challenge and desires to become a need filler.

22. Never write a retaliatory letter. You are not going to win by defending yourself. People who are your enemies will not be turned into friends by logic. The wise leader will not allow himself to be drawn into a battle of words on paper. The Devil knows that when he gets a leader to yield to temptation, he is not merely getting the leader

HOW TO TREAT YOUR PEOPLE

but all of those over whom the leader has influence.

23. Do not take your burdens or your problems to the pulpit. In the same respect, do not attack or retaliate from the pulpit. Do not spread gossip from the pulpit. One of the reasons why I do not fight back is because most of the time I am not aware of any fights. My people do not need a defeated me; they need a victorious me. Therefore, I need to be around victory throughout the week. A leader will come nearer to winning his battle by not fighting his battle. Don't get me wrong, leaders fight. Paul said in II Timothy 4:7, *"I have fought a good fight, I have finished my course, I have kept the faith."* Dr. John Rice could say, "I fought the battles." Lester Roloff could say, "I went to jail while fighting a good fight." In other words, the leader chooses which battles to fight.

The wise leader will feed his people from the pulpit, not burden them. He will come nearer to defeating his enemy by ignoring them. God didn't call a man of God for self-defense; He called the man of God for His defense. II Chronicles 20:15 says, *"...for the battle is not your's, but God's."*

> "Man's greatest need is to have a need."
>
> – Dr. Jack Hyles

CHAPTER EIGHT

Principles for Building Successful Relationships

PROBABLY ONE OF the biggest problems in churches today is the church-school relationship. The following are principles we have followed at First Baptist Church and the Hammond Baptist Schools. Setting principles alleviates the necessity of constantly solving problems.
• Seventy-five percent of the Sunday school teachers must be non-school related.
• No deacon can be school related. First Baptist Church of Hammond is a layman-controlled church.
• Church members who choose to send their children to another school are not treated as second-class citizens.
• Keep the church finances and the school finances separate. Every school must pay for itself. Do not take from the surplus account or from the surplus in any budget item to pay for another budget item.
• Each school should have a different location.
• School administration, faculty, and staff must be involved in the church.
• School administration, faculty, and staff must turn in an activity report.
• School administration, faculty, and staff cannot

Principles of Leadership

expel or suspend a student. The rules made by the deacons expel a student. The deacons set the amount of penalty for each infraction. A rule not enforced is no rule at all.
- The pastor approves everything.
- The pastor is the pastor; he is not on-site at the schools.
- The parents have a right to appeal any decision. The pastor never listens to an appeal alone.
- School administration may not do school business at church.
- The church schedule comes first, even if a school activity was planned first.
- No homework is assigned or tests given after a soul-winning marathon, Pastors' School, Christian Womanhood Spectacular, Youth Revival, the Valentine Banquet, or the Mother-Daughter Banquet.
- All full-time employees of the school must enroll their children as students in the school.
- Strict dress codes must be enforced in the school.

PUBLIC RELATION PROBLEMS can arise between the church and neighborhood. The following are principles we have followed at First Baptist Church and the Hammond area.

1. Visit every family in the church when taking a new church within the first few days of accepting the pastorate of the church.
2. Visit every downtown place of business.
3. Visit every house in the city you pastor.
4. Start a radio broadcast. Have a happy program and prayer time. I called ours, "The Pastor's Study." The goal of having a radio station is to permeate your city with the friendliness of the pastor. When "The Pastor's Study" aired in Hammond, from 9:00 a.m. to 9:30 a.m., often between 50 to 60 prayer requests were called in daily.

Principles for Building...

5. When taking possession of a new building, host a meal. Invite all of the neighbors within a two-block radius. Take complaints and explain your plans to neighbors. Say, "If there is ever a problem, please let us know." Do not assume an adversarial position in your neighborhood. First Baptist Church sent delegates to the houses around Hyles-Anderson College to let them know they had a right to voice any complaint, and they received a promise that problems would be corrected.

6. Have a banquet for the city officials. Prepare a program that welcomes them with singing, etc.

7. Stay in constant contact with the fire chief. Have the officials help keep your buildings safe.

8. Keep a good relationship with all government officials.

PUBLIC RELATION PROBLEMS can arise with and between church members.

1. **When the problem concerns a teenager who makes a mistake:**
   a. The first statement should be, "Tell me your side of the story."
   b. The teen should hear a statement such as the following: "You are a good teen who has done wrong."

2. **When the problem concerns a teenager who runs away:**
   a. Stay the teen's buddy.
   b. Do your best to keep the teen's relationship with his parents intact.

3. **When the problem concerns a situation with a child being born out of wedlock:**
   a. Say, "You're still my kids. You're young. If you

keep the baby, you will not finish school. You will be tied down. Give up the baby for adoption."
  b. If the expectant mother's parents are unsaved, meet with her each week to help her and encourage her.
  c. After the birth of the baby, counsel her to help her reach her full potential.
4. **When the problem involves an unsaved husband:**
  a. Call the husband and tell him you have found flaws in his wife and need his help to fix them.
  b. This statement usually brings a husband to the pastor's office. Be hard on the wife to win the confidence of the unsaved husband.
5. **When the problem concerns a student expelled from the school:**
  a. Hire a teacher (not from school) to tutor these young people at home.
  b. At the end of the semester, take pizza and host a party.
6. **When the problem involves a student or students doing wrong, but the school has no rule against the wrongdoing:**
  a. Call a meeting with the parents and say, "Your children have done wrong, but there is no rule. You parents will have to decide what the punishment will be."
  b. Have a vote.
7. **If the problem involves a divorce settlement, salvage everything you can out of everyone you can.**
8. **When the situation involves a widow or widower:**
  a. Offer advice about finances.
  b. Help put the life back together.

Principles for Building...

9. **How to preach the funeral of someone who has grievously sinned:**
   a. In a ten-round fight, eight rounds win the fight.
   b. In school, the student who earns all "A's" and one "F" still passes.
10. **Never vote anyone out of the church.**

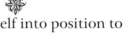

A LEADER MUST get himself into position to receive God's blessings. Proper ethics does just that. I Corinthians 15:33 says, *"...evil communications corrupt good manners."* A leader must set proper ethical principles.
- Never counsel with any woman more than twice in six months.
- Never visit any member of another Bible-believing church.
- Make no appointment with a member of another church without written permission from his pastor.
- Don't try to hire someone without first checking with the person's pastor.
- Don't hire a worker without a good reference from his former employer.
- I will not ordain a man to preach who goes to his home area to start a church to rival his home church.
- I will cut ties when I leave a church.
- Don't talk to a prospective student at a church that has a college.
- Don't read the name of an area church from which new members transfer.
- Don't make hospital visits to members of other churches.
- Treat your predecessor ethically.

FINANCIAL PROBLEMS CAN arise within the church. The leader should be transparent financially. Establishing proper

Principles of Leadership

financial principles alleviates the necessity of constantly solving problems. There are many common mistakes made by leaders. The following is a list of important financial principles to follow:
1. Don't spend on projected income.
2. Don't borrow on a projected income.
3. Don't have too large a percentage of the budget going toward indebtedness. Twenty-five percent should be the maximum amount.
4. You need a surplus and a budget.
5. Don't have the same people count money every week.
6. The pastor should not sign the checks.
7. The leader should be accountable to the people for the spending of their money.
8. The leader should not know how much the people give individually.
9. A purchase order should be filled out for every expense.
10. Know how to raise money. I have used the following strategy to raise money.
    a. Ask your wife how much you can give.
    b. Go to the staff, explain the burden, and see how much they can give.
    c. Go to the deacons, Sunday school teachers, and small groups of people within the church with the same approach.
    d. Ask the people to give 2% more than the tithe.

Relationship problems can arise with and between staff members. Establishing principles alleviates the necessity of constantly solving problems.
- I have never asked a staff member to resign.
- I have never fired, but I have fined.

Principles for Building...

- I have transferred unproductive people from one area to another.
- I have transferred people with personality clashes from one area to another.
- I have transferred people because of health problems.
- I have helped unpopular staff members become popular with the people.
- I come to the rescue of a staff member when he gets in trouble.
- I never publicly cross a staff member.
- If an undesirable staff member resigns, I replace him quickly before he changes his mind.
- I live by the principle that patience will often solve the problem.
- I do not contradict staff while counseling.
- I don't have to be first.
- I do not hire talent; I hire character.
- I hire potential and not just present ability.
- I do not hire new converts.
- I do not often hire people from the pew.
- I do not hire anyone who has caused trouble.
- I do not underestimate the popularity of a staff member.
- I ask for help from the staff in making policies.
- I study each staff member and treat him according to how he wants to be treated.
- I have regular staff meetings. I meet on Thursday afternoons with everyone. On the second and fourth Saturdays, I meet with the staff men. On Tuesday afternoon, I meet with the college staff and faculty.
- In gathering workers and hiring staff, I work on "growing" my own; I build my workers from within our ranks.

Principles of Leadership

- I give each staff member an area of responsibility.

THE FOLLOWING ARE personal principles I follow to help me stay on top. Again, establishing principles alleviates the necessity of constantly solving problems.

1. I do not allow discouraging statements, nor do I listen to bad reports.
2. I never look at the records of those who have transferred their membership.
3. I avoid negative people.
4. I never talk about church problems with my wife at home.
5. I do not get involved in others' squabbles with fellow preachers.
6. I give every problem a chance to solve itself.
7. I do not attack individuals publicly.
8. I do not drop a bomb unless it is to save the church.
9. I try to institute a change gradually.
10. I accept some changes.
11. When I have made an obvious mistake, I admit it.
12. When a battle is over, I do not preach against enemies.
13. I am a gentleman to those who choose to leave. I keep the door open because some may return.

CHAPTER NINE

The Importance of Counseling

EVERY PERSON SHOULD have a cabinet of counselors. That cabinet should include the person's pastor, a true friend, someone successful in his chosen field, one or both parents, and a wise person (a soul winner). The Word of God reveals much about a person receiving good counsel or bad counsel.

1. **Bad counsel brings tragedy.** *"Behold, these caused the children of Israel, through the counsel of Balaam, to commit trespass against the LORD in the matter of Peor, and there was a plague among the congregation of the LORD."* (Numbers 31:16)

2. **A nation was rebuked for being void of counsel.** *"For they are a nation void of counsel, neither is there any understanding in them."* (Deuteronomy 32:28)

3. **Imprudent counsel brings destruction.** *"But he forsook the counsel of the old men, which they had given him, and consulted with the young men that were grown up with him, and which stood before him."* (I Kings 12:8)

4. **Foolish counsel can cause death.** I Chronicles 10:13 says, *"So Saul died for his transgression which he committed against the LORD, even against the word of the LORD, which he kept not, and also for asking counsel of one that had a familiar spirit, to enquire of it."*

5. **Prudent counsel brings depth.** *"Counsel in the*

[81]

heart of man is like deep water; but a man of understanding will draw it out." (Proverbs 20:5)

6. **Prudent counsel confirms decisions.** *"Every purpose is established by counsel: and with good advice make war."* (Proverbs 20:18)

7. **Wise people listen to prudent counsel.** *"The way of a fool is right in his own eyes: but he that hearkeneth unto counsel is wise."* (Proverbs 12:15)

8. **A lack of counsel often fosters failure.** *"Without counsel purposes are disappointed: but in the multitude of counsellors they are established."* (Proverbs 15:22)

9. **Accepting prudent counsel brings lasting wisdom.** *"Hear counsel, and receive instruction, that thou mayest be wise in thy latter end."* (Proverbs 19:20)

10. **Counseling was a ministry of Jesus.** *"For unto us a child is born, unto us a son is given: and the government shall be upon his shoulder: and his name shall be called Wonderful, Counsellor, The mighty God, The everlasting Father, The Prince of Peace."* (Isaiah 9:6)

Prudent counseling can change the course of a person's life, change the course of a family, change the course of a nation, and impact a world. The wise leader will never underestimate a counseling appointment!

CHAPTER TEN

Preparation for Counseling

BEFORE A LEADER can meet the needs of his people in personal counseling, he must prepare himself. Probably 50 percent of his counseling will cover the subjects of marriage, child rearing, and finances.

The ritual I follow for every set counseling block of time is to claim God's promises and beg for His wisdom. I pray for each name on the list of my counseling schedule. I think of each person individually, and I pray for wisdom. The following are steps I follow in preparing and equipping myself to be an effective counselor:

1. **I constantly ask God for wisdom.** James 1:5 says, *"If any of you lack wisdom, let him ask of God, that giveth to all men liberally, and upbraideth not; and it shall be given him."* Tarrying with God to find the answers is what is missing most often in the lives of those who counsel. I spend time in prayer before the actual counseling session.

2. **I go soul winning.** Proverbs 11:30 says, *"The fruit of the righteous is a tree of life; and he that winneth souls is wise."* I do more personal soul winning when I need extra wisdom for counseling.

3. **I read to become knowledgeable about many subjects.** I must program this computer I call my brain. I always have something with me to read; I never know when

[83]

Principles of Leadership

someone might be late to an appointment. I never know when I might be in a traffic jam or stopped by a long train.

If most counseling deals with marriage, children, and finances, then logic dictates to especially read books and materials on those subjects. Some of the books I recommend are *The Home* by Dr. John R. Rice, and my series on *How to Rear Infants, How to Rear Children,* and *How to Rear Teenagers.*

For newspaper reading, I recommend reading the *USA Today*. I first take out the "Entertainment" section and throw it away. I recommend reading newspaper editorials. When I travel, I read the newspaper of the area where I am visiting.

I recommend reading magazines, such as *U.S. News and World Report.*

I recommend reading history books. Outside of the Bible and biographies, reading history has helped me more than anything else I have read.

I recommend reading biographies. Read to acquire their character, not their theology or doctrine. For instance, neither John Wesley nor Charles Finney were Baptists. John Calvin and Martin Luther were great men, but the truth is, if they were alive today, they would probably be fighting us. Their theology was a reformation theology; Baptist doctrine goes back to New Testament times, not just to the Reformation. Don't read their sermons; read about their lives.

I recommend reading geography books to learn about the nation and the world.

Read and re-read question-and-answer books. Dr. John R. Rice has two such books; William Pettingale has one. These books should be in every leader's library. I recommend reading one every six months for general knowledge. Spend more time on the practical questions than doctrinal

questions. A leader wants to learn what will help his people.
   4. **I live in the Bible.** I read it more than I study it. I spend a minimum of ten hours a week in Bible study.
   5. **I personally seek counsel.** The leader who encourages and comforts his people sometimes does not know what to do and needs a pastor also. Write down the advice you receive. Do not be afraid to ask another if you gave the right counsel.
   6. **Listen to the radio.** Listen to a news station, and be aware of what is happening in the world around you. Listen to good music as a subtle background.
   7. **Be around all classes of people and all races of people.** A church cannot be built entirely on the bus ministry. Keep in mind that a church is doing only as well as the drive-in crowd. Every leader must seek to reach middle-class America.
   8. **I think about the person with whom I will be counseling and the person's situation.** I ask God to give me love for that person. I ask God to help me realize that the person who always seems to know what to do sometimes doesn't know what to do. That is why that person is seeking advice.

Some Basic Principles I Try to Utilize:

• **I try to preach to the needs of the people.** Doing so will prevent much counseling. I often say from the pulpit that if the people will listen carefully, much of what I say will help them with the day-to-day situations of life.
• **I use letters whenever possible to help cut my counseling load.** I even use personalized form letters.
• **When I am out of my office and someone**

approaches me for help, I often say, "Can I talk to you right now?" Oftentimes, we can come to a good solution in just a couple of minutes.

• **I use the concept of having a "line" form after church services.** Again, many problems can be solved in a matter of a couple of minutes. If not, I schedule another time with the individual. I do no major counseling at this time. I plan to see people quickly, one after another, and allot approximately three minutes to each person.

• **I never make an appointment for the same day unless it is a dire emergency.** Usually, I wait up to three days, for I have found that most wounds heal themselves if they are left alone.

• **When I see that my people have problems and do not seek advice, I try to decide how I would advise them if and when I am asked.** I do not give advice if I am not asked.

• **I do not counsel with people if they tell me that they have counseled with others and they tell me with whom they have counseled.** I will counsel only that person when the previous counselor gives his permission for me to do so.

Procedures I Follow During a Counseling Session:

1. If more than one person is in the appointment, I listen to both sides before dispensing advice.
2. I do not pre-decide my advice.
3. I give each person the opportunity to tell his side of the story.

PREPARATION FOR COUNSELING

Kinds of Counseling

Most counseling sessions fit into one of the following categories:
• **Decision Counseling.** This kind of counseling involves people who are facing a decision in the normal routine of life, such as whom to date, which car or house to buy, or which job offer to accept. Generally, this kind of counseling can be done after a church service.
• **Marital Counseling.** I believe this kind of counseling should be done by appointment. No less than one hour should be given with both parties present. One spouse waits while the leader counsels the other; then the parties switch. Ask the one if the other's accusations are true. The final few minutes should be a time of giving advice with both the husband and wife present.
• **Advice Counseling.** I generally allot 15 minutes per appointment for this type of counseling. I call these the situations of life that people do not know how to handle, such as strife.
• **Rebuilding Counseling.** I do this kind of counseling on a regular weekly basis. I never give rebuilding appointments to women. As a matter of fact, I have no regular, week-after-week appointments with women. If a woman needs rebuilding appointments, encourage her to meet with a godly woman, or have your wife present.
• **Preventive Counseling or Public Counseling.** As the leader, I try to figure out what the needs of his people are and then preach on those areas. I discover the needs of my people by keeping track of my counseling appointments with my people. People should be encouraged to read books as a preventive measure.
• **Spontaneous Counseling.** I alluded to this type of counseling previously. If you sense that you can handle a sit-

uation quickly in two or three minutes, try to meet that need at that time.

- **Counseling by Mail.** I refuse to counsel about major problems by mail. I cannot know all of the ramifications of the situation. I promise to pray for the person and his situation. I use form letters in this type of situation.
- **Regular Counseling.** I spend time looking at the report cards of children who have no father in the home. Sometimes I spend a little time helping someone learn another tip about preaching. I also include rebuilding counseling as a part of my regular counseling.
- **Refereeing Counseling.** When I do this type of counseling, I persuade people to agree to do what I recommend. I tell them not to gripe at each other for one week. I ask them to write down their grievances and bring them to me. I do not see them again if they do not come to their appointments.
- **Check-up Counseling.** I see certain people regularly to check on their progress in the areas in which I have counseled them. I see them every two weeks for two months and then every week for six months.
- **Prayer Counseling.** The leader meets regularly to pray for people each day to help them have the victory that day.
- **Telephone Counseling.** I counsel via the telephone only in on-the-spot emergency counseling.
- **Group Counseling.** Talk to people who have the same group interest on a particular matter.
- **Senior Appointments.** I recommend having an appointment with every high school senior at some time during his senior year. Though I ask the senior what his plans are, I do not give any unsolicited advice.
- **Premarital Counseling.** I cover some expedient subjects in this area of counseling. For instance, I tell them

the four major causes of divorce are troubles in the area of money, sexual matters, in-laws, and child discipline. I also offer to explain to the young man the facts of life. I advise young ladies to counsel with a lady counselor. Often, I try to find the right counselor for her. I require them to read some books on marriage, including *The Act of Marriage* by Tim LaHaye.

- **Testimony Counseling.** Much of this type of counseling is done from the pulpit. When I preach to my people, I include testimonies of victories in others' lives that they need to hear.
- **Seeking Advice Counseling.** Ask the person seeking counsel, "What would you do if...." Then cite the situation about which you would like to know his thinking.
- **Third-Person Counseling.** I use this type of counseling to tell someone about a counseling session I had with another individual that fits their situation, but without the person knowing or realizing that I am offering advice. I make a reference to the area in which the person needs help by referring to another person.
- **Cooperative Counseling.** In this kind of counseling, perhaps I will call a father to "ask his advice" concerning his daughter staying in school when he has made it known that he wants his daughter to leave school. In so doing, I make that father a part of the decision.

When the Leader Needs to Seek Personal Counsel

1. The leader should never seek counsel from his members about personal matters.
2. The leader may seek counsel about his personal business.

Principles of Leadership

3. The leader should not seek counsel regularly from the same person or persons. He should not create a system that will not function when the participants are gone.
4. The leader should read, read, and read more, especially biographies.
5. The leader should never confess a sin to another unless he has personally wronged that person. He should not confess beyond the area that the sin is known.
6. A leader should never trust the confidentiality of anyone in the world. If he needs sympathy, he should seek it from Jesus alone.
7. A leader should seek counsel from his children about ways to counsel other children and teens. Doing so will bring him closer to his children and make them feel needed. The leader should seek counsel from his children regarding obvious matters. What a wonderful way to make them feel needed and close to their father!
8. A leader should not seek counsel from his wife unless it is in her area of expertise. If a leader seeks counsel from his wife, he should then use her counsel.
9. A leader should seek professional counsel only from another who is further along in his field.
10. A leader should not bring home problems to his wife. A woman cannot carry the load that a man can carry because a woman is made to be a follower. If she greets him at the door and asks, "Do you have a problem?" the right response is, "No, I have a church, and when I look at you, I forget what problems are!"
11. A leader should not lead by seeking sympathy. The followers will respond at first, but not later if the leader keeps asking. A leader is in his position to meet the needs of his followers. One of the most difficult concepts for a pastor to accept is that he is voted on every Sunday. His people come for sympathy and strength. Leadership gives

strength; it does not take it from the followers. Along the same line, do not share your burdens with anyone just to get sympathy.

12. A leader should never let his burdens become obvious. Instead, he should focus on others' burdens and forget his. He should run as fast as he can continue to run.

13. A leader should not share critical letters—publicly or privately. I never read anonymous letters. I do not continue to read a letter once I have discovered that it is of a critical nature. When a leader is tempted to feel sorry for himself, he cannot help someone else. If God cannot see you through the tough times, you shouldn't be seen through the tough times.

14. A leader should seek counsel concerning how to counsel a difficult matter. Do not be afraid to reschedule the appointment while you seek help from another.

15. A leader should learn to counsel with himself. Keep in mind that most depression is caused by an irregular schedule. Ask yourself if your down times come at any particular time of the day, week, or month. Ask yourself if there is a rhythm to your times of depression. A leader must work to keep his rhythm.

16. A leader should beg God to control his mind as he constantly asks for wisdom.

Bible Examples of Those Who Sought Counsel:

- **Manoah, a father.** *"Then Manoah intreated the LORD, and said, O my Lord, let the man of God which thou didst send come again unto us, and teach us what we shall do unto the child that shall be born."* (Judges 13:8) Manoah came to God's man for advice on how to rear his son Samson. The truth is,

Principles of Leadership

Samson was one of the great spiritual giants of the Bible. Of him, it is said, *"the Spirit of the Lord came upon him,"* more than of any other man in the Old Testament. Samson was brilliant. He thought of the idea of tying together the tails of 300 foxes, setting them on fire, and letting them loose in the grainfields of the Philistines. He was strong. He took the jawbone of a donkey and killed 1,000 men. He was a great leader. For 20 years, he ruled Israel as a judge. No president ever held office that long in the United States!

- **Saul, a son.** *"Then said Saul to his servant, Well said; come, let us go. So they went unto the city where the man of God was."* (I Samuel 9:10) Saul sought help from Samuel to find his father's lost donkeys.
- **David, a king.** I Chronicles 27:33 says, *"And Ahithophel was the king's counsellor: and Hushai the Archite was the king's companion."* David surrounded himself with older, experienced men as his counselors.
- **Benhadad, a king of Syria.** *"And the king said unto Hazael, Take a present in thine hand, and go, meet the man of God, and enquire of the Lord by him, saying, Shall I recover of this disease?"* (II Kings 8:8) Benhadad sent a request to Elisha by the hand of his servant.
- **The Shunammite woman, a mother.** *"And she called unto her husband, and said, Send me, I pray thee, one of the young men, and one of the asses, that I may run to the man of God, and come again."* (II Kings 4:22) The Shunammite mother was seeking help from Elisha for her dying son.
- **Jehoshaphat, a king.** *"But Jehoshaphat said, Is there not here a prophet of the Lord, that we may enquire of the Lord by him? And one of the king of Israel's servants answered and said, Here is Elisha the son of Shaphat, which poured water on the hands of Elijah. And Jehoshaphat said, The word of the Lord is with him. So the king of Israel and Jehoshaphat and the king of Edom went down to him."* (II Kings 3:11, 12) Three kings met with

Preparation for Counseling

the man of God to resolve a political decision.
- **Artaxerxes, a king of Syria.** *"Forasmuch as thou art sent of the king, and of his seven counsellors, to enquire concerning Judah and Jerusalem, according to the law of thy God which is in thine hand;...And hath extended mercy unto me before the king, and his counsellors, and before all the king's mighty princes. And I was strengthened as the hand of the LORD my God was upon me, and I gathered together out of Israel chief men to go up with me."* (Ezra 7:14, 28) King Artaxerxes required the services of seven counselors.
- **Solomon, a king.** *"Where no counsel is, the people fall: but in the multitude of counsellors there is safety."* (Proverbs 11:14) *"Without counsel purposes are disappointed: but in the multitude of counsellors they are established."* (Proverbs 15:22) *"For by wise counsel thou shalt make thy war: and in multitude of counsellors there is safety."* (Proverbs 24:6)
- **Moses, a great leader.** *"And the LORD said unto Moses, Stretch out thine hand over the sea, that the waters may come again upon the Egyptians, upon their chariots, and upon their horsemen. And Moses stretched forth his hand over the sea, and the sea returned to his strength when the morning appeared; and the Egyptians fled against it; and the LORD overthrew the Egyptians in the midst of the sea."* (Exodus 14:26, 27) This account is just one of the many times Moses sought God for strength and direction.
- **Samuel, a boy.** *"That the LORD called Samuel: and he answered, Here am I. And the LORD came, and stood, and called as at other times, Samuel, Samuel. Then Samuel answered, Speak; for thy servant heareth."* (I Samuel 3:4, 10) God chose Samuel when he was a boy to do a great work in Israel.
- **Apollos, a young preacher.** *"And a certain Jew named Apollos, born at Alexandria, an eloquent man, and mighty in the scriptures, came to Ephesus. This man was instructed in the way of the Lord; and being fervent in the spirit, he spake and taught dili-*

Principles of Leadership

gently the things of the Lord, knowing only the baptism of John. And he began to speak boldly in the synagogue: whom when Aquila and Priscilla had heard, they took him unto them, and expounded unto him the way of God more perfectly." (Acts 18:24-26) Aquila and Priscilla were used by God to counsel a young, zealous preacher boy.

Any leader who will take time to do an exhaustive Bible study will find many more examples of people who sought and followed counsel. These 11 examples were willing to be instructed. The prudent leader will seek counsel.

CHAPTER ELEVEN

Choosing Advice to Give

IN THIS PARTICULAR chapter, I would like to share principles I have developed in choosing what advice to give. A principle is based on a lifetime of learning. A person cannot afford to trust his immediate judgment; that is why I live by principles.

The following lists are decisions that I have found are almost always right to do, and not necessarily wrong not to do. I have found these principles generally to be the safe routes. Of course, I realize there can be an exception. I choose my advice by the following three principles:

1. If there is a Bible principle, let that principle make the decision.
2. If there is a Bible example, let the Bible example make the decision.
3. Finally, a leader should let his principles decide for him. The more his principles can make decisions, the fewer the opportunities for mistakes.

The following are principles I have developed, in no particular order, which have helped me in the decision-making process. The following are "nevers":
- Never advise a couple to get divorced.

Principles of Leadership

- Never advise two couples to become best friends. It is very unhealthy for couples to become too close.
- Never advise church members to go into business together.
- Never do second-person counseling.
- Never tell a man where he should go or whom he should marry. Only approve or veto a choice.
- Never advise a preacher to resign without a place to go.
- Never advise a man to be an assistant pastor in a new church.
- Never advise a layman to move because of a job opportunity or a job transfer.
- Never advise any student to change fundamental schools.
- Never advise a preacher to start a church with a split-off from a fundamental church.
- Never advise if not asked.
- Never advise anyone to marry until both parties are within one year of graduation from college.
- Never give advice when a decision has already been made.
- Never advise a divorced man to pastor.
- Never advise anyone to drop out of school for a season.
- Never advise a married couple to allow a teenager to come and live with them.
- Never believe an accusation, unless the accused one admits the wrongdoing, or you saw the wrongdoing. Why should I believe what I hear about you? Why should you believe what you hear about others?
- Never perform marriage ceremonies for unsaved people. Meet with them and try to win them to Christ. If they do not get saved at that time, do not marry them later.

Choosing Advice to Give

- Never advise people to follow a leader or man of God when he moves. God may then lead that leader to another ministry.
- Never give marital counseling if only one of the couple will come. Never advise divorce.

Some "Always" Principles in Counseling

1. **Always take the side of the leader or the authority.** Leadership is always for the authority.
2. **Always find both parties at some fault when you are mediating a disagreement.** No individual is ever totally wrong.
3. **I always advise, if there is any doubt, stay!** God led you where you are; He has not yet led you where you are considering going.
4. **Always advise a couple to have their first child no sooner than two years after marriage and no later than the wife's 30th birthday.** It is better for the last child to be born by the time the wife is 35 years of age.
5. **Always tell the wife that her husband is "#1" in her life.** Tell the husband that his wife is "#2." God made Adam to care for the Garden of Eden; He created Eve to care for Adam. If the wife has to work outside of the home, the husband needs to do part of her job.
6. **Always give a teenager the chance to be heard.** Tell him you will consider his position on a matter honestly and seriously. Do not interrupt him as he gives his side of the story. As a rule, this kind of courtesy is all that most teenagers want. I have often said that if a teenager had just one person who believed in him, he would not be lost to the world.

Principles of Leadership

General Counseling Principles

1. **If a young person chooses to attend a secular college, I give him three principles:**
   a. Never live in the college dormitories.
   b. Only attend a secular college with a nearby red-hot, soul-winning church. If there are none, stay close to home.
   c. I advise a ministerial student to attend only a Baptist college, not a non-denominational college or university.
2. **I advise only the adoption of infants.**
3. **I advise couples who do not have a child of their own to adopt.**
4. **If there is any doubt at all, I advise a couple not to marry.** Never work to decide if she is the right one or if now is the right time.
5. **I ask good people to wait six weeks before resigning a position.** I ask them to come back in six weeks, and if they still feel the same way, I accept the resignation. I have learned that many times their feelings will change.
6. **I suggest that couples marry within an age limit of no more than a 25-percent span in their ages,** such as 20 and 25, 28 and 35, 36 and 45, 40 and 50, 48 and 60, 60 and 75, etc. When I counseled with people with more than a 25-percent age difference, 78 percent of the time the situation went wrong.
7. **In a dispute between two people, always advise Party #1 to tell Party #2 what he thinks is right,** but do what Party #2 believes is right. In talking to Party #2, tell him just the opposite. Try to live by *"...in honour preferring one another."* (Romans 12:10)
8. **When a family is struggling, I teach the following concept:** Individual relationships in the home are more

Choosing Advice to Give

important than the family circle. Each person in the home should feel uniquely special to every other person. Each person should have time alone on a regular basis with every other person; one hour is a good time frame. I never counsel on marital problems without referring to this principle.

If there is no Bible principle or example, and none of the principles I have listed fit, I beg God to control my mind, then believe that He will, and I give the advice. When you advise, be honest as to your degree of certainty. Make statements such as, "I am certain," or "I feel good about this."

If you do not feel certain about a decision, ask for time to pray. Say, "I need time to pray," or "I need to get a second opinion," or "I don't know," or "I'd like to investigate."

If the problem is out of your area, such as a mental, legal, or physical problem, say, "I'd like to refer you to someone else."

Counseling Percentages

In my counseling, I find that the following percentages are fairly accurate in the four divisions of counseling:
Bible principles answer 25%.
Bible examples answer 10%.
Learned principles govern 50%.
Asking God to control my mind decides 15%.

Some Percentage Counseling Examples
- When a single person marries a divorced person, 65% end in failure.
- When a single person marries a divorced person with children, 95% end in failure.
- When an unsaved person marries a saved person, 97% of these marriages end in failure.

[99]

Principles of Leadership

- When a couple marries just to get married, 100% of these marriages end in failure.
- When a couple marries without pastoral approval, 91% of these marriages end in failure.
- When a couple marries without parental approval, 65% of these marriages end in failure.
- When a couple marries without pastoral and parental approval, 95% of these marriages end in failure.
- When a person with a moral background marries someone with a different type of background, 90% of these marriages end in failure.
- When a couple with different cultural backgrounds marry, 69% end in failure.
- When a college student drops out of college in the middle of semesters, 95% never finish college.
- When a college student drops out of college for a semester, 85% never finish college.
- Ninety-seven percent of college dropouts are not successful in the ministry.
- When a preacher does not attend Bible college, he generally never builds a big work.

CHAPTER TWELVE

Basic Principles of Counseling

COUNSELING WILL BE a big part of the ministry. The right kind of leadership inspires followship. People follow because of the qualities that they see in a person. Inevitably, the followers will need individualized help from their leader.

Office Decor, Manner, and Procedure

1. **The office should be decorated in good taste, with coordinating warm colors.** The designer should plan for good lighting, soft and well-placed fixtures. Always be aware of any unusual odors. The desk should look used but free of clutter. A few conversation pieces can help to break the ice. Kleenex should be readily available when needed.

2. **The leader should always be dressed appropriately for his counseling appointments.** A young leader should dress conservatively with a shirt and tie; if he is conducting business, he should also wear a sport coat or suit coat at those times.

3. **If possible, have two seating arrangements, one from which to conduct business and one for a relaxed setting.** Choose carefully at which seating arrangement to

Principles of Leadership

sit. I recommend starting at the informal place and move to the desk for business work. The leader should sit properly, somewhat casually for less formal appointments. The leader's posture will help relax the person seeking counsel.

4. Have a comfortable waiting room with some reading materials and refreshments available. The reading materials should not be controversial. Magazines would not be appropriate. A promotional flier about the church is acceptable.

5. If the appointment is with a business person, have some extras in the waiting room. Display the name of the person outside of the room on a board, give him a folder about the ministry, have someone to host him and serve refreshments, and give him a book as he leaves.

6. Handle businessmen with extra care; however, do not have an appointment with a businessman on a drop-in basis. Be sure to start his appointment exactly on time. Greet him with a firm handshake. Use his name often during the course of the appointment. Be interested in him as a person; after all, he is a human being, too. When you know a business person is coming for an appointment, learn all you can about him before he comes.

    a. When the businessman comes, tell him you have heard of him.

    b. Ask the businessman about his family; ask him if you can pray for him.

    c. I do not recommend witnessing to the businessman immediately. Let enough time pass for you to win his confidence. Sell yourself, slowly and tastefully.

    d. Be sure to have everything you need at hand. Plan in advance for the meeting.

    e. As he talks about his business, listen to every word intently.

    f. Do not try to be too humorous.

Basic Principles of Counseling

g. Have as a goal to become friends with the businessman.
h. When the appointment is over, walk out of the office with the business person. Introduce him to various staff members.
i. Immediately write him a thank-you letter for trusting you.

6. **When the person comes into your office, stay by your schedule.** Apologize if the appointment time is brief. Tell the person exactly how long you have for the appointment. Have a clock visible at all times to ensure you are staying on time.

Making Appointments

• First, determine your method of making appointments. I use the "Week-at-a-Glance" professional appointment book. When a person wishes to make an appointment, I ask that person to see my secretary in order to have his name put on a list. She later gives me that list; I schedule the time in my appointment book, and my secretary notifies the person of the time and date. My counseling is always conducted in my office; I never counsel at home.

• When the person asks for an appointment, I try to determine the length of the appointment based on the need. As a rule, marital problems require more time. My main goal is not to waste any time.

• When a person asks for an appointment, I ask the individual to bring a list of what he wants to discuss. Counseling time should be devoted to problems, not to doctrinal issues. Ask the person for the list so that you can control the appointment.

"There are two ways to be rich in life:
have what you want
or want you have."

– Dr. Jack Hyles

CHAPTER THIRTEEN

Kinds of Counseling

Marriage Counseling

IN THE CASE of premature marriage plans, I do not try to block a couple's plans. Instead, I try to postpone the plans. If I want a delay of six to eight months, I ask for eighteen months, and take nine!

Both the husband and wife should be present for marriage counseling. I recommend talking to them one at a time. Listen carefully to each person. Do not interrupt as each tells his side of the story. Make notes while listening to them. Ask, "What would you like to change about your spouse?"

Make two lists while taking notes. (1) Make suggestions as to what to advise, and (2) Write down questions to ask.

Generally, marital problems arise in four different areas: finances, in-law interference, love life, and the disciplining of children. Tell the couple that their problem is not uncommon. Tell the couple how you solved a similar problem. For instance, "When I disciplined or spanked our children, my wife went out for a while."

The wise leader always provides a prescription. Ask the wife to write down the prescription. Plan out eight to fifteen things they should do.

1. Divide the decision-making areas in the home.

Principles of Leadership

The fewer decisions a couple makes together the fewer chances there are a for a fuss.
   2. **Find a way for the wife to have several hours alone every week.**
   3. **Schedule a time each week for the couple to eat out together.**
   4. **Schedule a set time for the couple to enjoy some recreational time each week.**
   5. **Schedule times for the father to have regular weekly time with each child.**
   6. **Remind each person of the priorities of the husband and the wife.** God made man to care for the garden. God made woman to care for a man.

After the prescription has been written, repeat what has been written. Ask the husband and wife to promise to follow the prescription; even have them sign it. I recommend having some follow-up appointment(s) if it seems needed. Above all, make both the husband and wife feel that you have not ganged up on either one. Counsel using Bible principles, not Bible verses.

Counseling with Teenagers

Adults, too often, forget that a teenager is more an adult than a child. The greatest mistake adults make when dealing with teenagers is treating them like children. Teenagers misunderstand this method, and they withdraw. As Christians, they have no other recourse. The following are ways I counsel with teenagers:
- I do not become a teenager when I am counseling. I let the teenager become an adult.
- I let the teenager tell his side; too often he has no hearing at home. I do not interrupt the teenager or disagree

Kinds of Counseling

with him while he talks. I do not let the teenager give his side in front of his parents.
- I hear out the teenager, but I have him remain respectful. I do not believe or disbelieve what I am told.
- I take the teenager seriously. I do not make light of him or his statements. I do not categorize him with other teenagers.
- I tell the teenager things that will help him identify with me; I listen, but do not preach.
- I ask for his advice about the problem. I say, "What advice would you give someone in your situation?"
- I try to show the teenager the logic behind my counsel. I do not try to be too spiritual or too carnal.
- I let the teenager win on at least one point. I never seek to have a shut-out. Every teenager needs to be given the gift of dignity. If a leader finds a way to take the teenager's side in some way, the teenager will eventually come around and indict himself. Teenagers are very sensitive, and I have found that usually the more sensitive a person is, the more love he has.
- I never preach nor raise my voice. I always say, "I believe you are a good kid."
- I try to never take sides; the teenager comes for an appointment expecting to be ganged up on.
- I do not have my mind made up before the teenager comes to his appointment. If he knows that I am his friend, that may be all he needs to straighten up. Sometimes all a teen needs is someone who will listen to him. No young person would ever turn out bad if he had just one person who really cared. I want to be that person who really cares.
- I always give the teenager a choice between two good things when I advise him.
- I do not oppose the teenager's ideas; instead, I try to build upon them.

- I try to understand the teenager's problem and its cause. I let him know I feel for him.
- I expect only progress. I express positive feelings over a wee little change.
- I ask the teenager for his advice about some other problem or question having nothing to do with our appointment. I am building my confidence in the teenager, and he feels like he has helped me.
- I do not make the teenager's relationship with me hinge upon his taking my advice. I want to keep the lines of communication open in case I can help him in another way.
- I do not arrange for many orders to be given. I have found it is better to assign responsibilities and duties.
- When I see an infraction, I do not scold or punish immediately when the teenager does not do his work or fulfill his promises. Instead, I talk with him once a week about what he has done wrong.
- I try not to despair, but if I do, I would never let the teenager know of my despair.

Fairness in Counseling

Fairness to Other Men of God

1. Do not counsel with their members unless they have a letter from their pastor. The leader must be ethical concerning church matters.
2. Do not be one of many counselors.
3. Do not counsel contrary to another individual's advice.
4. Tell the person seeking advice, "If my advice differs from your pastor's advice, follow his."
5. Always stay on the side of the authority; do not believe accusations against fellow men of God.

KINDS OF COUNSELING

Fairness to the Person with Whom You Are Counseling
Before counseling, always beg God for wisdom.
• Do not counsel by mail or phone.
• Do not counsel when you are excessively weary.
• Do not make a person wait unnecessarily.
• Listen attentively to the person seeking counsel. Do not interrupt him. Take occasional notes.
• Treat the person seeking counsel with dignity and respect. Do not act superior to him.
• Hold everything said in a counseling appointment in the strictest of confidence.
• Do not decide in advance how you feel about the person seeking counsel. Do not allow his reputation to affect your decision.
• Look for good motives in any wrongdoing. Do not condemn the person, and do not preach at him. No one is always wrong. Before giving him your advice, tell him his good points.

Fairness to Others
1. Hear both sides of the situation.
2. Do not form an opinion after hearing just one side of the situation.
3. Do not counsel through a third party.
4. Only counsel when asked; otherwise, do not tell your views. Do not volunteer counsel.

Fairness to Your Family
1. Do not counsel in your home.
2. Give your family members appointments, too.

Fairness to Yourself
1. Only share in counsel those things that you want to

Principles of Leadership

be told. Do not trust anyone else to hold anything in the strictest of confidence.

2. Do not counsel in the homes of those seeking counsel.

Rebuilding Lives in Counseling

The Death of a Mate
1 The leader should be available to recommend an undertaker. He should suggest restraint in funeral expenses.

2. The leader should make himself available to help with the calling of family members. While he is at the home, he should take steps to help care for the food needs of the family by calling the appropriate person to help plan food delivery.

3. The leader should help the grieving ones plan the time, place, and music for the funeral service and help with the placing of a notice in the paper.

4. The leader should always make himself available to the grieving ones for counsel. At the cemetery, he should remind them of his availability to counsel.

5. The leader should go by the house in a week or two to offer his assistance again.

6. If the leader is asked for counsel, he should be sure to cover the following subjects, especially if he is counseling a widow:
    a. Where will she live?
    b. Is the dwelling too large?
    c. How much security does the house offer?
    d. How will the memories affect her?
    e. Can she adequately care for the house?
    f. Can she afford to remain in the house?

If indeed the answer to many of these questions is, "No,"

KINDS OF COUNSELING

discuss what realtor to call about her situation. Warn her about shady offers. Suggest she contact you or an attorney before making any decision.
7. Recommend a lawyer. Do not be a part of any transaction; simply recommend an attorney.
8. She should learn about wills, about investing money, about interest rates, about insurance, about terms and their meanings such as "prime rate," "certificates," and "government bonds."
9. The leader should discuss her life and her schedule. Questions should be asked such as:
 a. Will she need to fill void time?
 b. Will she need a job?
 c. Does she need full-time or part-time work?
10. The leader should find out if she needs friends.
11. Advise her to talk to her family members about your advice. Do not force anything; the leader's only role is that of giving advice.
12. Write her occasionally. Go by in a couple of months for a visit. Assure her of your continued prayers, and once again, offer her your services.

Reclaiming One from a Life of Sin
• The leader should plan to have regular visits with the person, possibly every week. The leader cannot meet regularly with a member of the opposite sex.
• The leader should seek to identify with the person seeking help. He should think of something he experienced that is similar to what the person seeking help has encountered.
• The leader should remind him of Bible characters who were salvaged from lives of sin. Take the time to share with him what God did with sinful men like David, Moses, Abraham, Jonah, Peter, John Mark, Noah, Job, and

Principles of Leadership

Jacob—just to name a few.
- Assure the person of God's forgiveness. Advise the person to claim the promise of God in I John 1:9 which says, *"If we confess our sins, he is faithful and just to forgive us our sins, and to cleanse us from all unrighteousness."*

"Let the wicked forsake his way, and the unrighteous man his thoughts: and let him return unto the LORD, and he will have mercy upon him; and to our God, for he will abundantly pardon." (Isaiah 55:7)

- Assure the person that he is still saved, according to I John 2:1; Romans 4:5; John 6:37; I Corinthians 3:12-15; and John 10:27-30.
- Assure him of your forgiveness. According to Romans 3:10; 3:12; 3:23; and Isaiah 53:6, all of us have sinned.
- Assure him of the forgiveness of most Christian people and church members. Warn him that some will not forgive and that he may receive some criticism. Warn him that the confidence of Christians must be re-earned.
- Warn him that he has forfeited some things. By that I mean, perhaps he has forfeited the perfect will of God for his life, but God also has an acceptable will for people.
- Warn him that he may sin again. *"My little children, these things write I unto you, that ye sin not. And if any man sin, we have an advocate with the Father, Jesus Christ the righteous."* (I John 2:1)
- Find one good friend for him.
- Persuade him to attend church activities and functions.
- Send a different person by his house every day to pray and read the Bible with him.
- Let him know that you do not expect total victory immediately. Tell him that you do expect growth. *"Be ye therefore perfect, even as your Father which is in heaven is perfect."*

KINDS OF COUNSELING

(Matthew 5:48) Let him know that he should expect only growth of himself, but warn him not to go too fast.

- Remind him to set a time every day to read the Bible. Remind him that he may not understand all that he reads, and he may not get much out of what he reads. Still, the principle of the dirty strainer holds true. Clean water draining through a dirty strainer produces a cleaner strainer. The more a person reads the Bible, the cleaner his mind becomes. Remind him of the importance of spending time with God every day.
- Remind him of the Holy Spirit and His availability according to Romans 8:9; I Corinthians 6:18-20; and II Corinthians 3:16, 17.
- Don't talk above him with spiritual vocabulary; use his vocabulary. Don't act like you are better than he is, and don't appear to be pious.

"He who preaches to broken hearts will never want for a congregation."

– Dr. Jack Hyles

CHAPTER FOURTEEN

Principles for Public Speaking

PUBLIC SPEAKING IS more than public speaking; it is privately speaking to individuals. For that reason alone, the leader must prepare himself emotionally: he should spend a few moments in meditation. He should think of the goal that he is trying to achieve for that service. He should picture himself at the judgment seat of Christ giving an account for the teaching or lack of it that he is about to do. He should approach the pulpit and stand before his people with a sober sense of awe, realizing that God is watching him and will someday judge him. May each of us give himself to whatever task God has called us to do.

Speaking at Funerals

Funerals are not a scriptural duty of a pastor, but a pastor is commanded to comfort people. *"Blessed be God, even the Father of our Lord Jesus Christ, the Father of mercies, and the God of all comfort; Who comforteth us in all our tribulation, that we may be able to comfort them which are in any trouble, by the comfort wherewith we ourselves are comforted of God."* (II Corinthians 1:3, 4) The leader has to do the things well that his people want him to do well so they will let him do the things they

Principles of Leadership

do not like. For instance, most people at First Baptist Church of Hammond do not actually like invitation time; it is a dead time for most of them. The same is true of baptism. The soul-winning program is not the most popular program. I believe that the way I have conducted weddings and funerals helped "save my neck" when I became the pastor of First Baptist Church. The most beautiful wedding and the most comforting funeral should be the ones held at fundamental churches.

In order to prepare well for conducting funerals, here are some personal things you should do immediately after the death of a loved one.

1. **Remember the times you spent together. Doing so will warm your heart.** Try only to think well of the person who is now gone.

2. **Get a picture of the deceased person and look at it for a while.** You have to feel in your heart that you miss him by giving special thoughts and time to him.

3. **Research the life of the person.** Take out the person's file and read some letters he has written to you. Keep in mind that you owe it to the family to love the deceased person. Talk to the person's friends. *(Do not let the family know you are researching about their loved one.)*
   a. Talk to his neighbors, his fellow workers, past friends, past fellow students.
   b. Try to learn about the good he did.
   c. Try to learn about his good qualities and his good habits.
   d. Try to discover his tastes and what he loved.
   e. Try to find out about some of his sayings.
   f. Try to find out the details of his salvation story.

A minimum of four hours should be spent on research and preparation for every funeral sermon.

Principles for Public Speaking

4. If possible, try to hear his voice on tape.
5. Late at night, drive by the place where he lived. Park outside the house and hurt for the family. The people need me to comfort them, so I must be in the emotional state where I can do that. Also, drive to a place where you share a memory with the person.
6. Think how you would feel if you lost the same loved one. If you have been through the same kind of loss, remember when you were in the grieving one's shoes. People need someone to empathize, sympathize, and care with them. Someone has said that a sympathetic heart is like a spring of pure water bursting forth from the mountainside. The leader needs to work at sitting where they are sitting and feeling what they are feeling. No one has a knack for caring about others; it is plain hard work!
7. Keep in mind that the service is mainly for the bereaved. The purpose of the funeral service is to comfort the family and to lend dignity to the departed. The main reason why I believe in funeral services is because that is where and when the family and others realize death is real. The leader should not let the family choose the funeral text; however, he can use a special verse within his sermon at some point.
8. The sermon should be representative of what the congregation would say. In your researching, find out what they would say, and then say it!
9. The sermon should never be negative. The leader should not take advantage of a "captive" audience. He should not use the funeral service as his forum to preach a message on Hell.
10. Be only mildly evangelistic. You will win more souls later this way.
11. The leader should walk confidently to the pulpit. He should stand erect and confident, use proper gram-

mar, and be precise and brief in his presentation. The funeral message should be 12 to 20 minutes in length. He should always plan to make some direct reference to the family.

    12. **The leader must prepare himself to be inspired from within.** There is nothing "deader" than a funeral crowd. He cannot depend upon audience inspiration. He should use few if any gestures. He should not break down and weep. Humor is out of order, unless it is in extremely good taste.

    13. He should speak very briefly at the graveside and then pray.

    14. The funeral service should be taped, and the family should be given a copy.

Sample Funeral Texts and Some Brief Outlines.
Genesis 50:26, *"So Joseph died, being an hundred and ten years old: and they embalmed him, and he was put in a coffin in Egypt."* The word, *coffin,* means "hope chest." Genesis 50:26 is a good funeral sermon for a good Christian.

Genesis 49:33, *"And when Jacob had made an end of commanding his sons, he gathered up his feet into the bed, and yielded up the ghost, and was gathered unto his people."* This text is a good funeral sermon for a member of a close family.

II Samuel 1:23, *"Saul and Jonathan were lovely and pleasant in their lives, and in their death they were not divided: they were swifter than eagles, they were stronger than lions."* This text is a good funeral message when two people die together.

John 14:1-3, *"Let not your heart be troubled: ye believe in God, believe also in me. In my Father's house are many mansions: if it were not so, I would have told you. I go to prepare a place for you.*

PRINCIPLES FOR PUBLIC SPEAKING

And if I go and prepare a place for you, I will come again, and receive you unto myself; that where I am, there ye may be also." This text is for the funeral of a saved person. I call this God's cure for heart trouble.

Psalm 91:1, *"He that dwelleth in the secret place of the most High shall abide under the shadow of the Almighty."* This text can be used for the funeral of an unsaved person, so the bereaved ones can be helped.

Philippians 1:21-23, *"For to me to live is Christ, and to die is gain. But if I live in the flesh, this is the fruit of my labour: yet what I shall choose I wot not. For I am in a strait betwixt two, having a desire to depart, and to be with Christ; which is far better."* This text is for the funeral of a saved person. List all that the person has gained.

II Samuel 12:23, *"But now he is dead, wherefore should I fast? can I bring him back again? I shall go to him, but he shall not return to me."* This text can be used for the funeral of a child.

Job 13:15, *"Though he slay me, yet will I trust in him: but I will maintain mine own ways before him."* This text can be used for a sudden, unexpected tragedy.

I Thessalonians 4:13, *"But I would not have you to be ignorant, brethren, concerning them which are asleep, that ye sorrow not, even as others which have no hope."* This text can be used to comfort those who take the loss especially hard.

Romans 8:28, *"And we know that all things work together for good to them that love God, to them who are the called according to his purpose."* This text can be used when the situation is particularly hard to accept.

Principles of Leadership

II Corinthians 5:8, *"We are confident, I say, and willing rather to be absent from the body, and to be present with the Lord."* This text can be used to comfort when the situation involves someone who wanted to die. In the case of a suicide, give something very positive about the person.

If the funeral is for a relatively unknown person in the church such as a mission man, mention his importance to the Lord and all that God did for him. Build him, not because of what he did, but because of who he was in God's eyes.

The Wedding Service

Just like funerals, conducting a wedding is not a biblical pastoral responsibility. There is nothing in the Bible about a pastor conducting a wedding or a funeral. (At least at a funeral, the pastor does preach.) I believe God's men have succumbed to the depravity of present-day society by seeing the performing of weddings as a pastoral duty. There is not much that a leader can do at a wedding that is spiritual and ethical.

1. **A wedding is simply good P.R. (public relations).** Probably nothing that a leader does can accomplish the building of good public relations like a wedding.
2. **A wedding is probably the only service a pastor conducts where he should primarily please the people.** In other words, a wedding is the only place a leader can pussyfoot and get away with it.
3. **A wedding is the only service that should be formal and traditional.** People who come to weddings expecting certain traditions to be upheld and followed.
4. **A wedding is the only service where a leader**

Principles for Public Speaking

should work to make people like him. Most people who do not like your preaching come to not like it. If you can make people like you at a wedding, they may return for the preaching services.

5. **A wedding is not the time for preaching, a Bible study, or an evangelistic service.** Neither is it a time for eloquence or speech making. I do not believe a wedding is the time to take advantage of a captive audience; rather, it is better to teach the Bible to the bride and the groom in the privacy of your office.

6. **Mild advice may be given at a wedding.**

7. **I would not suggest that humor be used at a wedding.**

Preparing for the Wedding Ceremony

- I try to give four hours in preparation for every wedding.
- I research the couple's romance and courtship. Find out about the first time they saw each other and how they met. Find out how they realized they were made for each other. Find out about the first "I love you." Research the circumstances surrounding the proposal. Determine their good qualities.
- I get alone and relive my experiences with the couple. If I can think of one, I go to a place that we have shared. That is my actively working on my love for the couple. (If I could give to future pastors or anyone, for that matter, anything I have, I would give them my awareness of what is happening.)
- I meditate on their hardships. One problem that leadership has is that many a leader does not have enough character to think about what is happening around him.
- I always look at their pictures.

Principles of Leadership

- I think of past weddings that I have attended. I try to think of what I liked about them, what I did not like, and what was left out. Beautiful weddings are made by a preacher who cares enough to prepare. I picture the newlyweds listening to the tape of their wedding and saying, "I don't think anyone ever had a nicer wedding than we had."
- The leader should watch the congregation during the processional. He needs to find out who is in the audience. The degree of ritual used and the amount of humor used is decided during the scanning of the audience. Ask yourself, "What kind of spirit do I want to create?" I also spend a few minutes loving the parents.
- During the first song, think of the bigness of the occasion. Pray, and be very aware of your responsibility.
- I stand off to my right (at a slant), and I have the groom and bride stand off to my left (at a slant) so the congregation can see the couple. Speak slowly and be articulate; be conversational but deliberate.
- Give attention to the parents. In some way, say something kind about the parents.
- Have the couple look at each other during the vows. I say to the groom, "Would you repeat these vows after me and to Mary."
- I ask that no photographs be taken during the ceremony. From the first "Let us pray," to the last one, no pictures may be taken! Even the photographer sits down during the wedding itself. After the ceremony is over, the wedding is then reenacted for photographs, and the audience enjoys this time of reenactment.
- Make much of the exchanging of the rings. In fact, my favorite part of the ceremony is the exchanging of the rings. Talk about the "love" finger and its connection to the heart. You can also present one or more of the following thoughts:

Principles for Public Speaking

    a. The giving of rings is a symbol of assurance; all I have is yours.
    b. Research occasions for the giving of rings; those times constitute something special. For instance, the king's ring was his official seal, a seal of ownership. A ring often is the insignia of an office or position. Wearing a wedding ring is the highest office a woman can hold.
    c. Mention the symbols in a ring: gold symbolizes deity; the circle symbolizes eternity; the diamond symbolizes durability. The rings are a constant reminder of love.
    d. The ring symbolizes the fact that man is God's deputy in the home.
    e. A ring is a symbol of riches. *"For if there come unto your assembly a man with a gold ring, in goodly apparel...."* (James 2:2)

- Be very deliberate in pronouncing the couple husband and wife.
- Turn and face the couple during the recessional.
- Pray personally and silently for the newlyweds as they are walking down the aisle.
- Congratulate the parents. The preacher should go promptly to both sets of parents on both sides of the center aisle to congratulate them before the usher comes to the front to escort them out.
- If the bride and groom would like to have a Gospel presentation, use it after the exit of the newlyweds at the close of the actual ceremony, but just before you have the groom and bride return to the platform for the reenactment photography. (Study *Hobb's Pastor's Manual*.) In everything you do, give it your very best.

PRINCIPLES OF LEADERSHIP

Miscellaneous
Special Services of Honor

Every leader must properly prepare himself for any kind of service. He must always keep in mind he is in fact privately speaking to many individuals sitting in the audience.

The leader must research and "do his homework" in order to be an effective leader and a vital participant in this special time of honor.

1. If the special services involves a graduation, research the graduating class.

2. If the special services involve an ordination, he should research the candidates being ordained.

3. He should research details about the building program, the land, plans, donors, contractor, architect, and be prepared for any questions.

4. He must realize what the occasion means to the people in attendance.

5. He should congratulate deserving people in his message.

6. He should thank those people behind the scenes. I seldom go anywhere to preach without going to the nursery and thanking the nursery workers. I thank each lady in the kitchen who cooks a banquet meal, and I shake her hand.

The following points relate to the speech you will make, not to the entire service:

1. Remember when you had your special service; be aware of the bigness and the importance of the occasion. Everything a leader does should be done properly.

2. Remember, a special service like this only happens once in the person's lifetime.

3. Remember, you are making memories for the person.

Principles for Public Speaking

Especially is this true of special services for teenagers.
   4. Think of the work that has been involved. Think of the distances traveled and all of the preparation.
   5. Think of the sacrifices that have been made. At one time I had the privilege of eating in my church members' homes. While I was there, in my mind I went through the process and details and preparation of my hosts.
   6. Look at the audience and imagine what they need you to be. Fall in love with the audience, and beg God to let you be what they need as individuals. If I love them, I can preach to them better.

The following points relate to the service itself.
- Stay within the allotted frame of time. Be concise and brief; 20 to 30 minutes is sufficient. Speaking over 40 minutes is a never!
- Dress conservatively. Have good posture. Be appropriate.
- Stay behind the pulpit. This is a speaking time, not a preaching time. Exhort, but do not rebuke. Do not crusade. For instance, speak for Christian schools, not against the public schools. Do not fight or try to fix anything.
- As the speaker, do not be too colorful and steal the show. It is not your day.

Ordination Outlines

I prepare a new message uniquely for each ordination service. Here are some samples.

Title: "There Is in This City a Man of God"
Text: I Samuel 9:6, *"And he said unto him, Behold now, there is in this city a man of God, and he is an honourable man; all that he saith cometh surely to pass: now let us go thither; peradventure*

he can shew us our way that we should go."
Outline: Look up the words, *man of God* in your concordance and find out what he did.

Title: "My Servant"
Text: Choose any number of verses dealing with servants.

Title: "The Preacher Ought to Be a Layman Who Lays"
Outline: Lay aside every weight. Lay up treasures. Lay by in store. Lay down your life. Lay hold on eternal life.

Title: "Titus, Stay in Crete"
Outline: Crete needs you. You need Crete. God needs you in Crete.

Commencement Outlines
Title: "Life's Choices"
Text: Ruth 1:16, 17, *"And Ruth said, Intreat me not to leave thee, or to return from following after thee: for whither thou goest, I will go; and where thou lodgest, I will lodge: thy people shall be my people, and thy God my God: Where thou diest, will I die, and there will I be buried: the LORD do so to me, and more also, if ought but death part thee and me."*
Outline: Ruth chose the Christian path. Ruth chose the Christian home. Ruth chose the Christian friends. Ruth chose the Christian God. Ruth chose the Christian death. Ruth chose the Christian burial.

Title: "Whatsoever Ye Do"
Text: Ecclesiastes 9:10, *"Whatsoever thy hand findeth to do, do it with thy might; for there is no work, nor device, nor knowledge, nor wisdom, in the grave, whither thou goest."* (Whatsoever ye do, do it with all your might.)

Principles for Public Speaking

I Corinthians 10:31, *"Whether therefore ye eat, or drink, or whatsoever ye do, do all to the glory of God."* (Whatsoever ye do, do it to the glory of God.)
Colossians 3:23, *"And whatsoever ye do, do it heartily, as to the Lord, and not unto men."* (Whatsoever ye do, do it heartily.)

Title: "How to Be Used by the King"
Text: Isaiah 40:3, *"The voice of him that crieth in the wilderness, Prepare ye the way of the LORD, make straight in the desert a highway for our God."*
Outline: Make the low places (depression) high. Make the high places (pride) low. Make the crooked places (dishonesty) straight. Make the rough places (Get sin out of your life!) plain.

Dedication Outlines
Title: "Furnishing the Building"
Show how the Tabernacle was furnished. The altar signifies preaching the blood. The golden candlesticks symbolize holding up Jesus. The table of shewbread signifies the Bread of Life (the Bible). The altar of incense symbolizes prayer.

Teaching a Sunday School Lesson

Keep in mind that the main purpose of a Sunday school class is to teach Bible principles. Sunday school is the fellowship part of church. If you are a Sunday school teacher, ask someone else to pick up your converts, perhaps your soul-winning partner. Be focused on your class.

1. Read at least ten times each passage you are going to teach. Write down your thoughts before you read a commentary, concordance, or a Bible dictionary.

Principles of Leadership

2. **Read the passage once looking for what I call "spice,"** such as Jesus, types, numbers, colors, symbols, and proper nouns. For example, in Luke 10:30-35, the following words are symbols:

Jerusalem	—	blessing
Jericho	—	cursing
"went down"	—	fall of man
thieves	—	Devil
raiment	—	salvation
"half dead"	—	spiritual death
"came down a certain priest"	—	priest is like you
Levite	—	caretaker of church
Samaritan	—	Jesus
oil	—	Holy Spirit
inn	—	church
two pence	—	paying the price

If you teach the "spice," people will love your Bible teaching. The main point however is always to remember that your neighbor is the one in need. Spice is like humor; it is not the main course.

3. **Read the passage with helps.** Use commentaries and/or Bible dictionaries.

4. **Read the passage with a list of your pupils at hand.** You need to study your pupils and know them. Write notes by their names. Make it a practice to find out what each lesson can do to help each student.

5. **Read the church-provided literature to be sure you are not in conflict with it.** This is not a time for your personal sermon preparation; you are a part of the team. Be a good team player!

6. **Greet every student as he enters your class.** The Sunday school hour is the only time a pastor has to win

PRINCIPLES FOR PUBLIC SPEAKING

the people to himself before preaching. I shook hands with everyone who came to church until my church had over 1,500 people in attendance! Being folksy helps people listen. The pastor cannot afford to hide in his study; he needs to be a part of Sunday school.

7. **Meet and introduce visitors to your people.**
8. **Introduce visitors properly in your classroom.** Write down pertinent facts about the visitors after you have talked to them. Then give the information when you are introducing the visitors, but do not read your notes. Remember that you are the visitor's first impression; be sure the visitors feel like royalty.
9. **Teach the lesson that the pastor prepares rather than using outside literature.** If outside literature has to be used, the lesson should be carefully edited. Teach the same lesson everyone else teaches. Spectacular teaching does not foster steady growth. The spectacular all too soon becomes the normal. Special subjects being taught in your class will affect other classes adversely. Build a church, not a class.
10. **Do not "preach" the Sunday school lesson.** The lesson should be taught like a Wednesday night Bible study.
11. **Do not be controversial, and do not be offensive.**
12. **Do not ask anyone to read, pray or speak, unless you have asked them beforehand.** Some people cannot read well enough to read publicly, and they would be embarrassed.
13. **Be the age of the pupils you teach; be what I call a "childish, juvenile adult."** (Please refer to chapter two in my book, *Grace and Truth*.)
14. **Teach your students from where they are, check into their activities, and parallel their personal experiences to the Bible lesson.** You are not necessarily

trying to leave your student with just one truth.
15. **Seek only limited participation; do not ask a question that requires an opinion.** Do not be dynamic.
16. **Most discipline problems in a small class are caused by ineffective teaching.** Teachers should allow at least 30 minutes to teach.
16. **Review and preview. Overlap from Sunday to Sunday.** The best visual aid is the expression on the faces of your students.
17. **Do not close Sunday school with prayer.** A prayer says, "It's all over." The day is not over, the morning preaching service is coming! Always be a part of the total picture.

Outside Speaking Engagements

One of the most amazing things is for a life to be transformed in one service. The speaker goes from being a stranger to being a life-changer in one sermon. There are seven steps to go through to be a life-changer.
1. The guest speaker comes to a meeting as a total stranger.
2. His first goal is to make his listeners like him.
3. Then, he must help them have confidence in him.
4. At that point, they will want to listen to him.
5. Then, the people can be captured by a truth.
6. At that point, they can be convicted.
7. A changed life is the result.

Principles About Accepting Speaking Engagements
• Do not accept an invitation where your presence might hurt and hinder. I believe everyone should be ethical.

Principles for Public Speaking

I believe it is unethical to preach someplace where your preaching could hurt what someone else has built.
- As a goal, always try to help the pastor of the work.
- There are some men I would have speak for me and vice versa. There are some men for whom I would speak, but I would not have them preach for me in my pulpit. There are some men for whom I would not speak; neither would they speak for me, but I would share a platform with them. No one knows who these men are. I try to follow my conviction. There can be no usefulness in trying to hurt another.
- I would recommend that every leader carefully read chapter four in my book, *Teaching on Preaching*.
- Do not choose a sermon on the basis of how well it went over at the last meeting.
- Choose a sermon with an "easy" invitation. For example, my sermon, "The Preeminence of Christ," is not practical enough for an invitation, but it is a good sermon for the times when you cannot give an invitation. Lives cannot be transformed unless the sermon has a "hook" in it. A sermon should never be an end in itself.
- Preach a sermon you enjoy.
- Keep a record of your sermons and where you preached them.
- After each Sunday sermon, consider it as a possible speaking engagement sermon. Ask yourself, "Could this sermon be a life-changing sermon?"
- Always be considerate of the speaker who is to follow you. If you are the first speaker, give no invitation, and be sure to stop on time.
- Do not be critical in your heart of anything you observed in the service. You must block out the negative, for you cannot preach if you feel critical! Don't let anything take your mind off what you are trying to accomplish.

- Do not try to have a mountaintop meeting. The purpose of this sermon is not to have a great service. The purpose is to transform lives.
- Use only spiritual humor; do not tell jokes.
- Do not plan on using the crowd to help you preach. Do not think they are dead if they do not shout, "Amen."
- As a speaker, blend the old and the new. Overlap the sermons the people have already heard. If you do not repeat something already said, you are making a mistake. You are also making a mistake if you repeat everything that has been said.
- Compliment the workers and the musicians where you preach.
- Start slowly and sincerely to convince the listeners that you are for real. Then outline your truth. Tell them what the first point is. As you preach, illustrate each point seriously, simply, and emotionally. Then close!

This last point about being a guest speaker is more important than all of the other 16 points combined.

Candidating for a Church

Before candidating, decide whether or not you are called to be a pastor or an assistant pastor. Some considerations are:

1. **Your age.** Normally, if you are under 25, you should start as an assistant. If you are over 35, start out in the pastorate. If you accept a position as an assistant and believe you may pastor some day, spend a minimum of five years serving the pastor as an assistant. You must be ethical to the investment the pastor has made in your life.

2. **Your years spent in a good church.** I was pastoring by the age of 21 because I grew up in church sitting on

Principles for Public Speaking

the front row right in front of the pastor.

3. **Your leadership ability.** Are you now able to lead people?

4. **The opportunity that arises.** This prospect should not be the one deciding factor, but it is a factor.

Before candidating, decide whether or not to start a church or go to an existing one. Some considerations are:

1. **Your age.** The older you are the less likely you are to start a church. Age 35 or less is preferable for starting a church.

2. **The time spent waiting for a call.** I usually advise a young college graduate to spend about six months looking for a church. If the Lord does not open an opportunity within that time frame, he should consider starting a church.

Before candidating, do not send resumes or write to well-known pastors. Contact only your best preacher friends, your home pastor, or a relative. Do not seek to pastor or be an assistant near your former church. Always take your wife with you when candidating.

Once you have been contacted and invited to come and preach, follow these principles for candidates.

- When asked any questions by the board or committee, the candidate must tell the truth.

- When he is asked a question by the board, the candidate should answer only what he is asked; he should not add anything else. He should let the board know the direction he plans to take and assure them of a gradual transition.

- He should moderate no general question-and-answer time from the pulpit. A candidate should not expose himself to public questioning from the entire church membership. Rather, he should answer questions only from the

Principles of Leadership

pulpit committee and deacons.

- The candidate should not enter into a popularity contest for the church. I would never appear to candidate unless I were the one being recommended as a candidate, especially if I were currently pastoring a church.

The proper way for a church to call a candidate is to nominate a pulpit committee, find the man, and then bring him to the church with a recommendation.

- The candidate should not tell the church people all that he believes. He can show them the highway he plans to travel, but not all of the towns along the way. Spiritual people can tell much about a person and his beliefs by the message he preaches. Unspiritual people cannot, so they will not oppose you. A leader changes a church by the way he administers medicine—in small doses. If the leader gives the whole bottle at once, he is stupid; on the other hand, if he never eventually gives them the whole bottle, he is a compromiser.

- The candidate cannot expect the church people to believe all that he believes. God may send him to that particular church to make that church into his kind of church. Fight one battle at a time; fight one issue at a time, or you will have several groups against you at one time.

- The candidate should carefully read the church constitution and articles of faith. He does not have to agree with the church constitution; he is just sizing up the magnitude of the battle he will have on his hands if he accepts the pastorate. He should consider pastoring a convention church only if that church agrees to come his way.

- The candidate should check on the financial condition of the church. He should learn everything he can about the church while candidating.

- The candidate can backhand sin without preaching against it in his candidating sermon. He can say something

PRINCIPLES FOR PUBLIC SPEAKING

like, "You are not saved because you quit your adultery, quit your drinking, or quit your smoking."
- The candidate should not mention money, parsonage, or other provisions. Instead, he should let his needs be what his income can provide. Mrs. Hyles and I were married for three years before owning a car.
- The candidate cannot afford to join anyone in criticism. In all of the years I pastored at First Baptist Church of Hammond, Indiana, I never criticized my predecessor. The same people who criticized him have since been critical of me.

When the Church Issues a Call

1. Insist on being the moderator of the church. Ask to moderate the church business meetings.
2. Insist that the pulpit is yours. You choose the guest speakers and who speaks in your pulpit.
3. Insist that the church staff is responsible to you.

It is best not to achieve these requests by an ultimatum. Simply ask when the call comes, "Who is the moderator?" "Will the pulpit belong to the preacher?" "To whom will staff members be responsible?" If the answers are unacceptable, simply ask, "Can that be changed?"

Suggested Candidating Messages

Title: "Redigging the Wells"
Text: Genesis 26:18a, *"And Isaac digged again the wells of water which they had digged in the days of Abraham his father."*

Isaac re-dug the old wells that had been filled in by the enemy. Billy Sunday re-dug some wells. D. L. Moody re-dug some wells.

Principles of Leadership

Title: "I Believe God"
We are both looking each other over. Let me help you decide. I believe God, the virgin birth, the second coming of Christ, the Bible is the Word of God, etc.

Title: "Removing the Landmarks"
Corrupt people moved the landmarks over slowly, a little bit at a time. The Bible is a landmark.

Title: "Seek Ye the Old Paths"
Follow the path of righteousness.

Conclusion

AT TIMES, LEADERS weep in the dark hours. At times, leaders spend sleepless nights. At times, leaders worry, fret, and sometimes think their ministries are over. At times, leaders doubt and then preach on having faith. At times, leaders have troubled hearts and then preach on John 14. At times, leaders worry and then preach on Romans 8:28. At times, leaders are afraid but then alleviate the fears of others. At times, leaders preach on joy while being sad. At times, leaders bind up the brokenhearted while broken. At times, leaders add the burdens of others to their own. At times, leaders convince their followers that God will supply all their needs and sometimes worry about their own needs being supplied.

Still, there is no way a leader can serve God without serving people. A leader's life has to be totally consumed with the needs of others. Every facet of the ministry dictates that the leader, the man of God, must live the selfless life.